If You Survived 7th Grade, You Can Be an Actor

Applying the Meisner Technique to Get Outta Your Head in Acting and in Life

Matthew Corozine

With Ruochen Shen

MCS Publishing
NEW YORK, NEW YORK

Copyright © 2021 by Matthew Corozine

All rights reserved. No part of this publication may be reproduced, distributed or transmitted in any form or by any means, without prior written permission.

Author – Matthew Corozine (with Ruochen Shen)
Developmental Editor – Joshua Rivedal
Cover Art – Mallory Rock, Rock Solid Book Design www.RockSolidBookDesign.com
Front Cover Photo – David Gazzo
Back Cover Photo – Hannah Davis

MCS Publishing
357 W. 36th St., Suite #202
New York, NY 10018
www.matthewcorozinestudio.com

If You Survived 7th Grade, You Can Be an Actor / Matthew Corozine.
-- 1st ed.
ISBN 978-1-7356171-0-7

"Over the past 20 years I have witnessed Matthew Corozine and his studio thrive and grow. His training ground has been my first recommendation for actors pursuing Broadway careers who want the most authentic training for their craft. I highly recommend *If You Survived 7th Grade...* It is a terrific primer for actors, as well as anyone who craves a fully realized, vital life."
- Sue Gilad, multiple Tony Award winning Broadway producer

"Groundbreaking theater practitioners from Sanford Meisner to David Mamet have reiterated the notion that acting problems are just living problems, and Corozine's book fully embraces this idea. When you talk to one of his students, even if only for a few minutes, it becomes immediately clear that this is a teacher who inspires and changes lives."
- Mark Deklin, actor and fight director, TV's *Designated Survivor* and *The Good Fight*

"This book not only teaches helpful acting skills and techniques, but also allows those who read it to apply to their daily lives and live better for it!" -Jackie Evancho, platinum recording artist, actor, finalist *America's Got Talent*

For Beverly Z. Davis. Who saw me at age twenty-eight when I could not see my own self. Knowing I would never fit in, Bev made me realize I belonged, was part of, not separate from, and helped me lead from that space so I could eventually use that to create a clearing in others to do the same. I went from surviving to thriving. Because of Bev's belief in me, I took on my calling and purpose and created Matthew Corozine Studio (MCS)—a creative home for myself and other "black sheep" who needed to belong and not just fit in.

Larry Rogowsky, who did it first and is always in my corner,

Brenda, for making videos and starting my book,

Ruochen Shen, who helped create it, shape it, and complete it,

Alain, for loving me no matter what I do and not being impressed with anything I do but being proud of me—faults and all. I love you, Alain. You and Mimmo are my family,

Daniela Lattes, for showing true friendship and being my family,

Tessa Faye, for always coaching me and being in my corner,

Sheri Sanders, for your love and support,

Nikki MacCallum, for inspiring me,

Ryan Tofil, for your loyalty and love—always,

Matt Clemons, Trevor McWhirter, and Trevor Markanovic—my super assistants,

Cooper Grodin, for being the real deal,
Terria Joseph, your continual love, trust, and support through the years,
All my MCS team in NYC, DC, and Miami
April Magen, for her integrity, taking a stand for me and helping me create what I speak,
Miss Kim, for always hiring me as a director and teacher and being part of my family,
my mom and dad—love you,
Susan Isaacs, Suzanne Cerreta, Danielle Jordan, Conor M. Hamill, Madison Edwards, Chris Russell, Christine Desimas, Kathy Deitch, Samuel Ladd Brinker, Lisa Bruno, Orietta Crispino, Nicole D'Angelo, Joshua Rivedal—all your advice, talent, instincts, and for getting me, Soho House Miami, Ali and Luke, my social media team, Rachel Schur, Tsu Tsu Stanton, Annie Chadwick, Mel Mattos, Rachel Policar, David Gazzo, Chelsea Feltman, Sara Romanello, Nathan Nolen Edwards, Gilbert Costache,
All the actors, assistants, admins, writers, and producers I have collaborated, coached, directed, taught, and loved in over twenty-one years of teaching, coaching, and directing.

CONTENTS

INTRODUCTION..1
THE BEGINNING (A VERY GOOD
   PLACE TO START) ACTING IS…......................5
A BRIEF BACKGROUND ON
   MEISNER AND MATT..11
A LITTLE MORE ABOUT ME AND
   EVEN *MORE* ABOUT YOU...................................19
LIVING, BEHAVING, AND BREATHING
   —A SOLID FOUNDATION...................................27
WHAT ARE YOU GIVING UP?.....................................31
THE REPETITION EXERCISE: 101..............................35
THE REPETITION EXERCISE: 201..............................43
PERSONAL MONOLOGUE EXERCISES.....................53
REAL-LIFE EXAMPLES OF
   PERSONAL MONOLOGUES..............................61
INDEPENDENT ACTIVITIES..69
COLD READINGS..83
EMOTIONAL PREP..89
CHARACTER WORK...103

REAL-LIFE CIRCUMSTANCES...................................107
SCENE WORK AND SPOON RIVER
       ANTHOLOGY.......................................117
IN CLOSING...121
ABOUT THE AUTHOR..133

INTRODUCTION

"For me, life is continuously being hungry. The meaning of life is not simply to exist, to survive, but to move ahead, to go up, to achieve, to conquer."

- Arnold Schwarzenegger

IF YOU'RE HUNGRY FOR MORE OUT OF LIFE. If you long to be more self-expressive and crave a fuller artistic and creative existence. If you have trapped the artist inside you, avoided the creative voice in you, and are coming from a place of shame. If you are someone who needs to be seen and heard more than everyday life can offer a person working hard for love while hanging on to the myth, "if X happens...I will finally be happy," you need to continue reading.

This book is for all kinds of actors—closeted actors, working actors, former actors, rehabilitated actors, wannabe actors, and should've-been actors. It's for social actors—those special souls who have been acting their whole life while hiding their true selves behind a mask while desperately hoping to be liked, seen, and heard. Maybe you're that closeted creative genius, and every time you walk by a Broadway marquee or see the opening credits of a TV show, you know your name should be up there too, right where it belongs.

What kind of actor are you? All of us have more than one kind of actor living inside us.

Whatever the kind of actor that lives inside you, you're here for a reason. There's an area, probably somewhere in the realm of show business, where you feel you're experiencing lack. And you've likely felt the effects of this deficiency for a long time. Now, you've decided to face that thing, that need, head-on. You're taking your control back. You're on a mission to become the actor you've always wanted and always known you can be. You may be a teenager, your early twenties, or even an older senior citizen and feel like the career of acting is calling. Maybe you know nothing about acting technique, but you are keenly aware there is a trapped actor-creator-creative spirit within you. If that is the case, I'm excited for you, and I'm here for you.

Join me and learn about the craft of acting. Get coached from the page, discover how to connect to be the best you, and unearth the actor inside you. Oh, and you'll also get some skills to get out of your own way in everyday life. This book and work will meet you where you are. If you've never taken an acting class or if you're a Broadway two-time Tony Award nominee who needs a push from good to great, this book is for *you*.

And just to be a little more relatable, and so the focus isn't on you all the time (who wants that 24/7, am I right?), I'm going to offer you little snippets of my personal story within these pages. These anecdotes will help get certain acting lessons across and may help you relate and feel less alone while on your acting journey.

Back in 2000, in New York City, when I was 28 years old, I took all my anxiety, fear, depression, shame, and panic and learned to own it and use it. No longer were these liabilities, but assets. I even turned them all into a superpower: vulnerability. This newfound self-accountability led me to explore and eliminate the secret I felt inside for a long time, that I wasn't okay as a person—and I built an acting studio from it.

THE BEGINNING
(A VERY GOOD PLACE TO START)
ACTING IS...

"Acting is living and behaving truthfully and fully under imaginary circumstances."

- Sanford Meisner, adapted by Matthew Corozine

THE OPPOSITE OF FANTASY IS REALITY. Most people have a limited belief system. This is a big reason why I love the Meisner work. You need to build imaginary circumstances and fantasy, but you have to pair it with being in the moment and dealing with whatever is happening truthfully. I work from this definition of acting—living truthfully and fully under imaginary circumstances. All my students memorize that in their first class. This is Sanford Meisner's definition, but I added the word "fully." Why? Because there's a fullness in allowing oneself to take part in a heightened reality that helps us break through areas we have neglected, hid from, or shut off. This heightened reality is essential in acting.

Everyone has an actor in them. A part of them that needs to be seen and heard and self-expressed that only has permission to do so in a heightened reality (what we call "the work" in imaginary circumstances). To get to the actor in us, we must unlearn the old story running the show of our life. We have to move past the old ways of needing constant control, our brains and lives on autopilot, and a self-limiting belief system to uncover the artist who has always been there. The Meisner Technique was eventually the key to the door that unlocked the artist in me that had been fighting to get out since childhood—and it can be for you too.

I first dabbled in this technique in undergrad at SUNY New Paltz and attacked it seriously in the late 1990s in New York City. When first starting out as an actor (several moons before I founded MCS), I had tons of acting teachers (or self-glorified critiquers as I now refer to them) who would say, "Matt, you're in your head." I would also hear things like, "Matt, you're not in the moment," or "we see you planning and working and anticipating outcomes. You're working for results." The worst was, "you're not listening," which is the kiss of death for an actor. Ouch. But nobody ever gave me tools or a technique to go beyond this. How the hell was I supposed to stop planning, get out of my head, and be in the moment?

I was stuck...like a used car that sometimes works, but really, there's no guarantee. Will the engine turn over? Will a young Matt deliver a good acting performance in class? Find out next on *Days of our Acting Lives.* I was truly struggling back in those days.

I liken my well-meaning acting coaches and teachers in my early twenties to a lifeguard telling a first-time swimmer, "Stop drowning! Can't you read the sign? It says *no drowning*! Stop it!" But how do I stop drowning? How would young Matt, and how can you stay in the moment?

The Meisner Technique was my lifeboat. I could focus on the technique rather than my life programming, my old story, and *trying* on my own through my own thinking. This did not work, and it never did. My best thinking got me to a place where I could not go further without a paradigm shift.

The Meisner Technique was that shift. It was the first time I felt okay not being okay. Growing up, I felt like I was one of the messier members of the human race, not unique or "special," and definitely someone who didn't belong. I began telling myself the story that I wasn't male enough like the other boys and I was inadequate. The experiences and emotions I recognized in my body were those that aren't the most pleasant, won't win you a superlative at the end of high school, and caused me unnecessary shame. Raise your hand if you've ever felt...awkward, shy, embarrassed, insecure, vulnerable, scared, angry, rageful, and/or like an asshole. These were and are all legitimate parts of myself, but I wanted no part of any of them, and I hated those parts of me. Thankfully, I found out through my Meisner training that these human parts of me needed to be included in every moment to be a good actor. To build this technique, I had to stop compartmentalizing, which was what I was doing since I was kid-Matt. I needed to start incorporating all the divided parts of me to be the artist I truly am.

Wait a second! All the stuff I hated about myself and hid was what I wanted and *needed*? Yes. It was the only way to have truth in my art and call myself an artist rather than a wind-up doll that "performed."

So, how does someone become divided, unwilling to own the parts of themselves they feel are "icky"? Why would a person compartmentalize? For a lot of reasons, but to help you understand, I'll briefly touch on my experiences as a younger man.

I grew up in a born-again Christian family in the 1970s and 80s in Peekskill, New York. (If you are my age or older, it was the same locale of the ol' hit TV show, *The Facts of Life*.) But I had a secret: my attraction to men. I was gay, and despite the anti-gay programming I received from all sides growing up, something inside me was okay with it. I knew it was considered wrong, and other people in my church and family did not feel a same-sex attraction like I did. So, I decided something had to be wrong with me. How could a butch-looking young man be so sensitive, effeminate, relate well to women, feel emotions strongly, and have such a keen sense of people lying and pretending and "acting" in life? Wrong, wrong, wrong. But I knew what was "right," which was a version of 1980s born-again Christianity that sprung from the sleepy American suburbs. And that twisted version of theology was also caked heavily in the terrible "S" word. Shame.

Shame can only thrive in secret, so I was the king of hiding. And kid-Matt had to cover it up by being the best, most special, most liked, most wanted, and most attractive. I had to have it all together and not need help. I needed to always portray a perfect version of myself and get out of situations quickly before people found out the real me. Shame cannot have connection, authenticity, and vulnerability—which are all the things necessary for relationships to thrive. So, I split. I hid parts of myself and committed to a "life of acting." Acting as if I was doing well all the time (of course, I wasn't). If my outer façade ever cracked (it did), I would panic and hide and start the shame-cycle all over again.

Fortunately, I survived and learned (more on all that later) and grew and found that the Meisner Technique could free me as an actor. But I also found that it could help me grow as a person.

You can do this too! Hell, if you survived seventh grade, you can be an actor. We all had to split on some level to survive seventh grade. To be the best actor you can be, you must connect to all the divided parts of yourself. Yes, you needed to split them off to survive childhood, but you're no longer in survival mode. It's time to thrive in life and as an actor.

Church. Family. Government. School. None of these gave me the truth of me. It was the Meisner work in the famous studios at Carnegie Hall that did for me.

So, let's go back in time…and get the story that was written in me and all of us. Let's write a new story for you and craft a new present life that can take you into the future you want to create.

This is what I do with all my students who walk into MCS to begin this work.

A BRIEF BACKGROUND ON MEISNER AND MATT

"If you ask me what I came to do in this world, I, an artist, will answer you: I am here to live out loud."

- Emile Zola, 19th century French novelist

IT'S IMPORTANT THAT YOU HAVE a little background on me and the work I do and the work you will be doing. When we know where we've been, we'll have a solid foundation to work from and a better sense of the direction we're going in.

While this need not strictly be a textbook on the Meisner Technique, you may wish some context about the Meisner work from Meisner himself. Though I have never taken a class with him, I know a thing or two about acting history dating back to the beginning of the twentieth century.

Sanford Meisner came out of the Group Theatre in the 1930s and 1940s in America. The Group Theatre was influenced by Stanislavsky and Russian realistic theater after seeing natural behavior on stage that was not burlesque, comic, or vaudeville. And this changed America. Soon, the Americans found out that the Russians rehearsed for four years. The Americans wanted to create a technique-based system that didn't take four years to do a play, which is not a financially sound business practice. And in today's world, quite frankly, you are lucky if you get four weeks.

From this desire to create a new acting technique, new methods of acting were developed in the 1930s and '40s by Group Theatre greats like Lee Strasburg, Stella Adler, Sanford Meisner, and Bobby Lewis. Some of them remained friends and supported each other. Others, such as Strasburg, who created a technique to use past experiences from your life, completely opposed Meisner. There is still controversy about these different techniques to this day.

Meisner developed his technique at the Neighborhood Playhouse. The Neighborhood Playhouse is still in existence today, and they still teach the Meisner Technique. From Meisner's work, various new teachers sprung up. My teacher, Mr. Modica, was one of them.

The family tree of the Meisner teachers is intriguing. There are now multitudes of Meisner teachers. I am probably the purest of what my teacher did, but not the purest Meisner teacher. Purists from the repetition world use repetition almost robotically from moment to moment. I took Modica's work and blended it with *The Artist's Way*, along with what I learned from Landmark Education, Tony Robbins, Bev Brumm (my SUNY New Paltz acting teacher), Brené Brown, Anne Lamott, Nadia Botlz-Weber, Dr. Joe Dispenza, Louis Howes, Hal Elrod, Ed Mylat, Jay Shetty, Russell Brand, *The Miracle Morning*, and many books and podcasts of great leaders, sports coaches, and people that teach mindset and patterns to help the actor get out of their head.

From 1995 to 1998, I took classes and studied with Robert X. Modica, who was Meisner's right-hand man for many years. Modica was a gruff man who taught us vulnerability and sensitivity. At that time, I needed a tough, masculine man to teach me this work.

Carnegie Hall, Room 809

Mr. Modica had American flags in his classroom and photos of the Korean War (in which he served) on the wall. Because he was a Marine, he would make us do cold readings of poems or messages from the Korean War and the Declaration of Independence. That is where I got the idea of creating a cold reading of poems and lyrics from pop songs and musical theatre. I developed the exercise from what Modica made us do. He used poems from D-Day, and I use Stephen Schwartz's lyrics from *Wicked*. Modica was incredibly patriotic and displayed some stereotypical tendencies many would associate with being from New York City and Italian.

Modica held class in the old-school Carnegie Hall studios in New York City. Modica was known to have a bit of a temper. He also loved you and cared about you as a teacher.

Mr. Modica was interested in seeing me grow, but not making me feel good. As a result, I grew in acting, and I started to feel better about myself from within. It was a good, long-lasting feeling and not the quick fix that the ego wants. It took me years to get to that place.

The Beginnings of MCS

In 2000, I had just finished directing a show. My company manager from that show told me, "You need to start a class the same way you run rehearsals." Back then, I was just teaching people to listen and react. I was doing the Meisner work I learned with Mr. Modica, who came from Sanford Meisner.

So, I started with one class a week while waiting tables on the side. Back then, I didn't know if I was ever going to get away from waiting tables. I was good friends, and still am, with Susan Isaacs, actor and writer of *Angry Conversations with God*. She was so encouraging and one day said, "Matt, you are going to be teaching full time in a year."

I needed someone to see that in me, because I couldn't see it myself. My friendship with Susan at the time was a kind of mentorship that I needed. We're kindred spirits.

I rented a small rehearsal studio and called some friends from college and some classmates from my old class. I charged very little money at the time. I was teaching people repetition, the beginning of doing Meisner work. I knew I had a gift to coach, that I was a director and a leader. But at that point, I didn't know what the hell I was doing. What drove me forward was the respect I held for the work. Repetition fascinated me the most. It felt as intriguing as having ESP or learning a foreign language. You can put your attention on someone and feel a connection with them through the subtext of the game. That experience gave me a thrill, and I loved it. I was hooked.

Back then, I made up a mock ad for the *Backstage* newspaper, "Meisner classes with Matthew Corozine." I had to build a home, a community, and I needed it badly. However, at the same time, my manager Tsu Tsu Stanton called me, in her signature raspy voice, "You have to pay for new actor headshots. You're almost out." Except, I didn't have money to place an ad *and* pay for new headshots. I had to take a risk, a big one at the time, and I decided to do the ad.

After I spent all my money on the ad and a studio rental to hold my classes, I never looked back. That decision marks the turning point of my career. That was when I built a community I always wanted to have.

Except, now I had to go to Modica and tell him I was teaching. It was scary. It was a little controversial for me to leave his class and start teaching at the age of twenty-eight.

It was an awkward conversation, and I didn't want to face his disapproval, but I knew I had to tell him the truth, just like he taught us to do.

At first, he was skeptical of my ability. My heart sank, and I wept. After hearing him speak for a bit, I finally found my voice. "Mr. Modica, you and your work have changed my life. I feel called to give back using that work. I'm so sorry if I hurt you. I'm so sorry if I am out of line. I *have to* teach this work."

He said nothing and just looked at me. Then he put his hand on my shoulder and hugged me. "You will succeed because of your heart. And you're allowed to come back on Friday nights anytime you want." It was then he knew that I understood the work because I found the ability to express myself. That was what he taught us: you speak up no matter what. And you tell the truth even if it's hard.

If I did not speak my mind before I left, I would have felt ashamed in front of Mr. Modica. I would have never stayed connected to him through the years.

Soon after that, I started to advertise and was eventually down to one day a week working at the restaurant. I was also getting busy with directing projects. One day, I went into the last restaurant I worked at on 44th Street and 10th Avenue. I was there, ready for my shift. I barely took shifts anymore, but I did not want to leave it entirely because I needed that weekly $150. Then they told me they took me off the schedule because I was never there. I walked out, and it struck me: I don't wait tables anymore. I'm an acting teacher. I started crying, and I called my best friend, Larry Rogowsky, Broadway producer and Tony Award winner. I asked, "Larry, what do I do now? Do I get another restaurant job?"

He said, "No. You go teach acting." I only had two classes a month then. I was not making any money. But Larry insisted I should teach my classes.

For the next two years, every Friday and Saturday night, which used to be my money-making shifts in New York, I would walk by restaurants packed with people, feeling guilt in my heart that I should be working in a restaurant. Old me growing into the true me. Then one day, one of my students, Kathy Deitch, booked a role in the original cast of *Wicked*, which helped establish my acting studio.

Over the past two decades, I have come full circle with many of my student actors. They've gone on to have brilliant careers in show business as TV, film, and Broadway actors, directors, and writers. But I'm most proud of who people become as they grow inside and outside of MCS. I'd like to think my students have learned a lot from me, but I've learned so much from them. Much like Mr. Modica and Susan Isaacs were mentors to me, I've been able to be a mentor to many others. And I hope that through this book and beyond, I'm able to help you and mentor you and usher you along your journey as an actor, artist, and outstanding human being.

A LITTLE MORE ABOUT ME AND EVEN *MORE* ABOUT YOU

"The formula of happiness and success is just being actually yourself, in the most vivid way possible."

- Meryl Streep, actor

WE HAVE AN AUTOMATIC WAY of being based on past stories, moments, and decisions. We subconsciously recreate our past (the brain is always looking for something familiar to connect to), then complain about how we want a new future. For many of us, there's an uncomfortability living in the present moment.

For example, when in an elevator with strangers, everyone feels nervous and awkward on some level. We all feel human weirdness in everyday situations. And yet, our society says there is an appropriate way to be, which dictates that we not express what is actually going on. We are conditioned to behave in certain ways—to be professional and logical, to do things proper based on etiquette. When we are in a conflict, we are taught to give evidence to support why we are right, rather than listening and looking at all sides.

Good acting involves breaking away from all of that—the learned behaviors of what makes you look good and what you think makes you look less stupid or pathetic.

When you move away from those preconceived notions, we will fall in love with you on stage (and likely off stage as well). Whenever Meryl Streep receives an award (will she ever stop?), she stumbles on her speech, trips, or may need to fix her bra strap. Those actions break the myth that she is always glamorous and infallible. We fall in love with her because she seems so human. This is smart and self-aware—she is being herself in a situation where people are supposed to behave differently. Many politicians do this too—they find a way to weasel into people's subconscious and appear strangely relatable. A dumb guy, a plain Jane, the people's princess or president.

In my family experience, I felt that acceptance and love were not unconditional. It was only conditional on not having problems and being entertaining. This wasn't a conscious decision from my parents. I knew deep down I was loved unconditionally, but I didn't *feel* it. Part of it had to do with the false narrative my brain created so I would be right (you're bad, Matt, you deserve to be rejected), which I had to unlearn as an adult.

But as a child, I felt that to receive love, I had to be perfect, good, funny, and special. That specialness messed me up. My dad was a musician, composer, and artist, so I felt like the child of a famous person, too. Sometimes, I got away with things because I was Vinny's kid—or got to skip steps or be on sports teams I didn't have the experience or the skill for. And that also screwed me because I never really learned. I get students at MCS, people who never learned how to lose, or be in pain, or were an only child and didn't fight with siblings. You need to be able to draw on those past painful experiences. The time you looked dumb or did something terribly embarrassing to you and your family. Your ego does not want people to see that you are actually bad at something you claim to be good at because you built an identity around it. But if you admit the truth, the painful stuff like accepting where you are in life is the only way to grow into the best you possible. Like the mall directory—you are here, but you need to go up two floors to Spencer's Gifts (can you tell I was an '80s kid?). You need to know where to start—*a la* the YOU ARE HERE sign at the mall—to get where you want to go. Are you willing to tell the truth and start there? Or are you going to keep covering it up?

I call it running from the cops. I use this reference a lot in my class. You go from town to town, changing your identity, but you can never be yourself. When you are constantly looking over your shoulder, knowing they are coming, the real you starts to emerge. To my students who put on this act, I always say, "The cost is too much and more painful than the payoff."

But getting rid of that false identity can also be scary. Because that is the automatic way actors reach out, and the brain cannot undo these old lies all on its own. It's a bit like an old friend who does you more harm than good. How many times have you told yourself, "I'm going to be vulnerable," or "I'm going to be different," but did not end up doing it? You can, however, act yourself into different thinking. You can't think yourself into good acting. Your best thinking got you here. But you need to be coached to get to the next level.

There are three areas we live in.
1. The stuff I know I know—how to make cookies, how to teach acting, how to swim.
2. The stuff I know I don't know—rocket science, how to build an aircraft, how to do brain surgery.
3. Then there is a whole world of stuff I didn't know that I didn't know. And that is the area that my coaching and our team at MCS focus on and want to uncover in you.

Finding Your True Self Through the Meisner Technique

In 2000, at age twenty-eight, MCS was created out of *need*, ignited by my friendship with Beverly Z. Davis and by doing "the work" training in the Meisner Technique with Mr. Robert X. Modica at Carnegie Hall Studios. I also had to get past a lifetime of shame, compartmentalization, anxiety, and depression. I felt so abandoned growing up. As a young kid, I was Christian, and I knew I was gay. I did not know where I belonged. Or how to reconcile those two worlds. Good boy vs. "bad" boy. Right vs. wrong. It felt like I had to reject myself to get through adolescence. I wanted to hide and play characters other than myself since I only knew rejection.

Through early adulthood, I kept living a pattern and story of rejection. I wanted to play other people and experience rejection so I could validate the story in my head. Humans have an inherent need to relieve the cognitive dissonance in their brains—opposing viewpoints that cause distress—to bring life back to order. In my young mind, I was bad for being gay and deserved to be rejected. And as such, I had to create conditions for my life to make that true. Not exactly healthy, but that's the human brain for ya!

This kind of mental "relief" I just described is actually opposite of being a great actor. The Meisner work I started doing in my twenties opened me up and changed that need within my life to believe and relieve that cognitive dissonance. It took me away from my self-limiting beliefs, and it will do the same for you. How many of us stay in an old definition of ourselves and have to keep proving it over and over and never grow? I know I'm not the only one.

After having created MCS, I started to learn how to be a great artist. The artistry of acting is not about playing other people. It is about playing the parts of oneself that split to survive childhood. I had trouble being my true self—partially out of shame and partially under pressure from the outside world. So, I tended to hide my feelings and tell myself, "Just look cool." Splitting and hiding is not something unique to being gay; it's universal. That is where the Meisner work comes into play, and through it, I found out—I am the character I want to play. Integrating my divided self is my art. This is similar to the integration of the divided self you had to do to survive seventh grade. So, for all the folks sitting in the back, let me say it louder. "If you survived seventh grade, you can be an actor."

Maybe you feel you don't need to connect to your sensitivities to be a great plumber or electrician—but you do. We all want to be around vulnerable people. We are attracted to people who let us truly see them, faults and all. To be a great actor, you have to be vulnerable. Connecting to every part of yourself is not only about becoming a great actor; it also helps you develop into a better person. Doing this work brings health and a boldness to live more fully on this planet. Living in the real world under the guise of acting has saved my life, so I want to impact other people to do the same thing. You don't have to be on TV or in a blockbuster film or on Broadway to do this work. In a sense, I teach acting by *not* teaching acting. I'm helping you unlearn the bad habits you have learned.

The Meisner work forms around what I knew was in me all along (like Dorothy at the end of *The Wizard of Oz*) and believed to be true but did not have language for. Learning Meisner taught me to surrender to the part of myself I had run from or decided wasn't worthy of being around.

Success leaves clues. Follow the great masters and their habits and techniques, then make them your own. That is what I did with the Meisner Technique. And it is just that—a set of drills. If you allow yourself to learn the rules and the truthful impulse of when to break said rules, you'll do great as an actor and as a human being. I came to thank the work for giving me a tool and language system to navigate through acting and life. When I discovered this, it was like Helen Keller at the well, learning how to spell and express the word "water."

I had no technique or tools to navigate life as a kid. I thought if I had enough faith, I would heal my secret sexuality and shame problem. It didn't work. Now, I have enough faith that living my truth (not denying parts of me) is the only way to live. And it makes me grateful for my painful past that caused me to be the man I am today.

Your journey to living your truth started when you picked up this book. This is your tool to unblock the actor, artist, and creative within—the true you. This book focuses specifically on unblocking your creativity by making you better at acting. We are going to remove your emotional blocks, resistance, and fear. The most exciting part about this work is there is a tangible technique. It's not just an acting technique, but something that can be translated into life too. My class has attracted many students who don't necessarily want to be actors—they are creative people who know an acting class will help in their work and life.

I always teach people from the future they cannot see. Most of the time, we are so clouded by our past. I am here to help bring people out of their past and into the present, so they can start creating a brilliant future for themselves as an artist. This work is an extension of a masterclass, an extension of meeting me, and an introduction to the world of moving forward in life…with acting. You will learn to integrate your past and not deny it by applying Meisner work, creating a new future you will love.

LIVING, BEHAVING, AND BREATHING—A SOLID FOUNDATION

"Most of the successful people I've known are the ones who do more listening than talking."

- Bernard Baruch, American statesman

LET'S START WHERE YOU ARE. Breathe. Make some noise in your chair. In fact, don't sit in the chair how you are conditioned to. Let a breath come out of you that matches what is going inside of you emotionally. See how your brain wants you to do this right, to perform and look good. Take your first risk in this work and let go of how you look and sound. When you let go of looking good, you actually end up looking great.

Purposely let out a gross sound accompanied by some kind of movement. And breathe. Breathing makes you feel. It brings up truthful behavior, which is what we are after.

Breathe.

Breath is the string, and the mind is the kite. The breath controls and moves the mind—you can recondition your thoughts now with your breath.

Let's add listening. To listen is a full-time job. Listening with the intent to learn and not to respond is incredibly difficult but doable. An actor's greatest skill is the art of listening. Without your agenda, without waiting to say your line, without wanting to fix the other person—to truly listen. Even right now, stop reading this and listen to sounds around you. The traffic outside your house, the air conditioner on the airplane, the noisy subway, the street sounds outside your apartment. You did this as you—not as Hamlet or some character. The character of *you* lived truthfully as you took in those noises, which came from listening.

From here, you can react instinctually without judgment or thought and take on a point of view of how you feel about what is happening. Maybe it's, "I love the sound of that bird. It made me smile," or "I hear my roommate slamming the door, and it bugs the hell out of me." You weren't judging what was coming up for you in the moment. You were doing, and you were simply "being."

Listening is the doing, the action. From full commitment to the action (listening), behavior starts to occur. Emotions are a byproduct of the action. When you truly listen, you'll notice that life and the world around you will always be different. The bird doesn't chirp the same way two times in a row. The garbage truck has different sounds each time it stops and collects trash. Your scene partner says their lines differently each time if they are in the moment. Even if your scene partner isn't in the moment, you can still listen and work off that which exists.

What if you took these principles and incorporated them into your life, your friendships, your work life, or your intimate partner life? What would that do for you and those around you? What would it look like if you integrated this work into your acting life? A whole new level of authenticity and creative genius opens up. Pretty exciting, no? Let's continue…

WHAT ARE YOU GIVING UP?

"Whether you think you can, or you think you can't—you're right."

- Henry Ford

WHAT DO YOU HAVE TO GIVE UP? I start all my seminars and most of my MCS classes with that very question. I want to ask you the same thing, and I'd like you to take some time with it and answer truthfully. Don't judge what comes up for you. Don't try to sound like someone you admire. Say what you need to.
- People who look like me don't get cast.
- I don't believe my dreams will come true.
- I disappoint and fail at everything.
- Everyone is out to get me.

- I don't belong.
- It's not fair.
- I don't get angry.
- I'm not good with money.
- I can't be an actor and make a living and have a family.

What usually comes up is a core belief (which deep down you may know isn't true) or a pattern of thinking the mind has developed to protect you from potential future pain. This soon-to-be old way of thinking is often negative or unhealthy but keeps you "safe" by allowing you to stay in what you know. Being aware of those self-limiting beliefs and speaking them aloud or writing them in a journal releases the hold they have on you. Just like shame, this old way of thinking can only live and thrive in secret. Once exposed, you find yourself more able to live in the present moment and the unknown—exactly where I want you to be as your coach.

Language has power. I love the word *abracadabra*, a semi-made-up term in magic. In the Aramaic language, it comes from a word that means, "I create like the word." In Hebrew, it is similar to a word that means, "I create as I speak." Through speaking into existence, we will give up our old beliefs, thoughts, and myths that stop us from developing into a future healthy version of ourselves. See yourself as the future you. Most of us live life in "cause and effect," meaning, "If X happens, I'll be happy." How about "causing an effect"? Find happiness and bring your desired life to you.

Your brain and body respond to your thoughts the same way it does to reality—it does not know the difference. That's why living under imaginary circumstances as an actor is so powerful. You are tricking your brain into a new belief system and way of being. Imagine what you want in the world. Your finances, career, acting, art, creative life, romantic life, friendships, family, how you love in the world, and how you show up in the world. Imagine you already have all that and *are* that. Feel what that feels like. If you take this on, what old way of being do you need to give up, or what way of thinking do you need to become this person now?

Maybe you have to give up the narrative that, "everything will always fall apart," "it never works out for me," "the other shoe will always drop," or "I can't be a successful actor and be wealthy at the same time." What self-limiting narratives and beliefs do you need to give up? What is at least one new narrative you need to take on to be the best vision of your future self?

The brain is always working to protect you. Uncover what is wrong or what aspect of your life needs some work or a fresh coat of paint, as it were. Ask questions. "If I change my narrative from X, the old way, to Y, the new way, what is the worst thing that could happen? Do I need to protect myself from this? What's the best thing that could happen? What happens if I don't go after what I want or need in my life?"

The truth is, you'll find out that you're safe and already protected and that if you don't go after what you want, let go of the old, and resolve to live in the present, you'll stagnate, and your soul will die a slow death. It's not the cutest answer, but I'm your coach, and I have to tell you the truth with love.

Stand up where you are, come on stage, and give up your old story. Tell us the real, true story of who you are. What are you willing to give up? It *has* to be control. Once you do, amazing things start to happen with your language, your breath, and the action you take. You're learning to become brave, taking on living in the unknown, and somewhere deep down, you're okay with that. And I, and we are proud of you for that. Do it for us because we need you, but most of all, do it for yourself—you and your art will be better for it.

THE REPETITION EXERCISE: 101

"The way to get started is to quit talking and begin doing."

- Walt Disney

YOU, AN ACTOR, ARE SEATED across from another actor. Both of you put your attention on each other. What is the first thing you get? Express that to your partner. The other person will repeat, and you will follow suit until one of you notices a change in the other person.

"You blinked."
"I blinked."
"You blinked."
"I blinked, and now you're laughing."
"Now, I'm laughing."

This is the very beginning of the repetition exercise. Let it come out of you organically. Irrationally, it will start to develop its own subtext. See how the brain loves to keep the words in the realm of what it thinks is logical. But simply repeat exactly what you hear.

There may be a slight shift in inflection in the words as you repeat, but only if you are not trying to control the exercise.

When I moderate the exercise in person, I'll then instruct, "When I say your name, pick up on something new that exists." You don't want to be theatrical about this or work for what you believe is interesting. Trust what you get from the other person. Maybe it's as little as, "You moved your hand." Don't make assumptions or conclusions while doing this, like, "You're nervous." Be honest and observant. What did you truly get in that moment? All you know is that they moved their hand. We don't know yet if they are actually nervous or have irritable bowel syndrome—which is why we don't want to make conclusions during the repetition exercise.

When doing the repetition exercise and leaning into its true purpose—to be observant of your partner and to just "be" in the present moment—it will ignite something in your inner life. As an actor, you start to work off your partner and begin to act and react based on what you are seeing and hearing, not what you are thinking. Little moments start to influence behavior. Instincts begin to grow, and we choose to now act on them or just observe them.

In acting, we have to be participating observers and let the sounds and behavior of the words in repetition start to affect us, build up, and become its own heightened reality. This can and will bring you to new truths. The more you let go of *you* and fall in love with the person you're working off of, the true *you* starts to emerge. And the true *you* is the most interesting and captivating *you* there is.

Why the Brain Fights the Repetition Exercise

Your brain wants to keep you from danger. It is looking for problems, so it can keep you safe. But what is safe for the ego? What is known? Is it your past? What is your past made of? Stories and decisions that keep you in the "known" so you can have things figured out and be in control. This world, this old way of doing things, is what I want to help you break away from. Only then can you live in the moment and respond using your instincts.

Be in the Unknown

The repetition exercise is the only technique that trains you to be in the moment and to "get outta your head." This phrase, also part of the book's title, is a signature phrase I say to my students all the time. The repetition game creates a clearing for spontaneous behavior to show up in an acting game. It's a way to get past ruminating thoughts or self-judgment or anything that takes you away from your scene partner or the present moment. When it comes to repetition exercise, Meisner, a classically trained pianist, describes it as the scales a pianist plays for practice. Through the repetition exercise, an actor works off the life of the other actor, not knowing how your words, actions, or behavior will come out. Isn't it scary to let the story evolve without you "helping it along" and forcing an outcome? You must give up working for results so you can be in the moment. How do we do that? By fully listening and getting your attention off yourself. In real life, we love to know and be right and be in control. We *must* give that up to find the actor in you. How? Through *listening*.

1. Get your attention off yourself.
2. Take what you're getting from your partner and work off of it. You want to be in tune with the sounds and behavior from the other person before the brain has time to qualify it or judge it. Act before you think, unlike how we were trained as kids to think before you act.
3. Do what is true in you. This is the essence of the technique and the muscle we are building

It is through repetition that we trick our brain, which always wants to look good. As a result, whenever I am at a workshop or seminar, I open my class by being vulnerable right away. I shake up traditional conventions a bit. I tell a brief story about myself that allows the room to connect with me. It's a bit like how Meryl Streep wants to mess up the little things in her acting work. Let the mouth stutter. Let the boobs sag. That is how she allows all of us to relate to her. It is only by letting your guard down and bringing all of yourself to each moment (not filtering out what you don't like or think is not useful), that you will become the great actor who already lives within you.

Let Your Instincts Do the Job

In my acting studio, an actor's first class begins with the repetition exercise, a famous exercise created by Sanford Meisner. It is so powerful that after twenty-one years of teaching it, I still have not gotten bored with it. It has become its own language.

The repetition exercise is also a major reason why Meisner had such a bad reputation. There have been teachers and acting classes that came after Meisner where actors got bullied and things got thrown. That's not what the exercise was intended for. There still needs to be some level of psychological safety in an acting class. I don't want to dismiss anyone who has had a bad experience with the repetition exercises in someone else's class. But it's possible to have something good (repetition, church, medicine) perverted by a bad facilitator or teacher. It's also possible to relearn while in a healthier environment.

The repetition exercise is a means to an end. It is one of the drills Meisner created to train actors to work from impulse rather than intellect, logic, or one's automatic socialized way of being. As the legend goes, one day, Meisner was talking to an elderly person in his life who was losing his hearing. The elderly man said, "What?" Every time he repeated it, he generated a different inflection. But he was not trying to make that difference intentionally.

You *can* try to make a different inflection every time you repeat to try and sound interesting. That is one way to be theatrical, but you are not being truthful. And you're working toward being truthful under imaginary circumstances. So, Meisner found that if people just repeat before thought and brain pattern come in, truth will come out of them from impulse. They do not have to memorize the script or think of the next line or what to say next because the repetition is the script. You don't change the words until the moment changes and a new moment is realized.

For example, if I say to you, "you are reading this sentence," you would repeat exactly what you hear. You won't have to memorize the next line because you'd simply be repeating, "you are reading this sentence." You don't have to think using memory. (Memory and language live in a different part of your brain than impulse and instinctive behavior.) Thoughts are the language of the brain, while emotions are the language of the body. Ultimately, as an actor doing Meisner work, you want to memorize lines (by rote, with no inflection) and then let them come out through an organic way of being in the moment of working off your partner—the sounds and the behavior, not the logic. You're trusting that all the background work is already there for you. You don't have to make it happen. Just let go, listen, and work off your partner. Yes, you will eventually be speaking a playwright's words, right? Recall the pinch and the ouch. You can't say "ouch" before the pinch. All acting is a reaction to something that has occurred. We are trying to get you to not "act" the line but respond as your true self. You have to re-train to become your full human self, because somewhere along our journey we forgot how. You have to unlearn life to live truthfully under imaginary circumstances.

Repetition is the training to read subtext. Don't think about the next line because you are going to repeat the line just said. Let it be informed by your partner's behavior. In fact, everything you do springs from your partner. You cannot do anything unless the other person makes you do it. Where does that come from? It comes from listening and responding before thought. Listening is a full-time job and demands all of you. You can't do two things fully in life (again, multitasking is a myth). Listening is how I train actors to "do" before "thought." It is physical, like being an athlete.

This is how we distract the brain from automatically trying to protect us from future pain (learned from past experiences). The brain learned to do this from past painful experiences, something it has done since we were young and didn't have the proper language or acting techniques. We all have layers of trauma associated with our story. The repetition work is a way to undo those.

THE REPETITION EXERCISE: 201

"Tell me with whom you associate, and I will tell you who you are."

- Johann Wolfgang von Goethe

THE FIRST FEW ROUNDS will have the two partners working off sounds and behavior (not logic of the words). I'll coach the partners to start by making "you" statements rather than "I" statements, going from 2nd person to 1st person. For example, "You took a big breath." The partner replies, "I took a big breath." The first partner repeats, "Yeah, you took a big breath." The second partner must include the "yeah," and it becomes, "Yeah, I took a big breath." Soon those words will lose their logic from observation and become behavior. This behavior may even look unreasonable compared to the words being said. That's okay.

There are three ways to change the repetition.
1. When a physical change occurs in your partner that strikes you in the moment. "You wiped your brow."
2. An emotional change occurs with your partner. "You're getting upset." Or
3. An emotional change occurs within yourself. "I feel so much love for you."

The other actor must repeat the change in repetition right away even if their brain is quicker than impulse (which will be starting to form new neural pathways to act before thinking). From the repetition exercise, the inner life of the actor will become activated, and it will start taking them places they didn't know existed. These are non-logical parts that come up when you let go of control and go off what you are hearing by allowing the repetition to wash over you. Amazing moments and lost parts of you start to emerge. The you that got split or divided starts to come together, and you start having reactions and behaviors that are different from the "real life you" who you have been playing. You are now conditioning the "true character of you," which is now "behaving truthfully under imaginary circumstances."

Action Is Attraction

You already learned the definition of acting is living and behaving truthfully, under imaginary circumstances. Living means doing. From this doing, you have impulses to act on that form the basis of our behaviors. In life, you can't act out all behaviors because it isn't always appropriate. It would be like kissing everyone or punching everyone, and you can't do that.

When you are doing something, you are in an action. People who take action are more attractive—especially when working with a partner and their attention is away from themselves and is in the present moment. When musicians are in the moment, they are fascinating to watch. If you watch somebody playing a sport or teaching and they love what they're doing, they are interesting to watch because they're immersed in their passion. They are living and behaving in action.

The word action is in the word attraction. The last six letters of attraction are "action." When you are in action, you look better—even though you are giving up caring about how you look. When we let go of trying to look good, we actually start to look good. A big part of MCS is letting go of looking good or how you sound. The only way to do that is to get your attention off yourself. You get there by being completely involved in action. As an exercise, I have my students imagine they are on stage by themselves, living and accepting they are at home and have nothing to do.

Nine times out of ten, the actor in the exercise releases a relaxing exhale. I'll then point out they're relaxing, which is not doing nothing. But from there, actors often struggle to figure out how to do nothing. Their mind starts wandering. If they know they are an acting class and everyone is watching them, their attention is no longer on the moment. However, a shift happens. The actor finally starts to give over to doing nothing, as opposed to acting like they are doing something or faking it. Watching this transformation, this person becomes so much more attractive.

The Meisner work builds a pathway to getting your attention off yourself, taking a new action, and having a new result—an imaginary circumstance. That is the first step. Something happens when you watch someone actually doing something as opposed to pretending. Accepting you have nothing to do is awkward, so you give yourself over to the action. Your face starts to change.

Who you are during the repetition exercise or in an acting class is not who you are in real life. I have learned as an adult to pause and learn about the person's inner world sometimes before I respond. I have learned that my happiness, joy, and who I am are all based on the future me I created. I do not approach real life in reactionary Meisner mode. Instead, I live in anticipation of all outcomes and create the me I want to show up as.

I train my brain that I already am the future me. I have to create the role of Matt and get rid of what my head does and says and not believe those thoughts. Sometimes *that* is only the truth of the moment.

On the other hand, I spent a lot of years where I felt my Meisner work was, "I need to tell everyone my truth!" That was the game I had to play because, for years, I split and denied my truth. Once I found my truth in my early twenties, I didn't want to go back to that anxious, insecure kid who needed to know he was okay. So, I replaced vulnerability and anxiety with perfectionism—an unhealthy and unhelpful substitute. I also created a new set of rules and belief systems for how people should behave. At that time, my favorite part was taking it upon myself to release anger on people who I felt were not doing what was right—I was always looking for a fight. And as we know, what you look for you will find. It is the reticular activating system (RAS) in your brain. It's the brain's need to validate your beliefs, regardless of whether your beliefs are right or healthy or useful to you. Unfortunately, the brain may filter out truly important information and leave you only with information that validates your belief system (even if it's unhealthy or non-useful). Through the RAS, the brain is simply trying to create order.

The repetition work trains you in subtext so you can respond from that part of your brain. This is where there is no thought, just impulse—some call it being "in the zone." It allows you to remove the part of your brain conditioned to how one would is or "should be" in conflict, to get you to be truthful, show up in it, react to it, and let the other person affect you. Anything you do is not up to you. It is up to the response of your partner. During the repetition exercise, if you repeat before thinking, words come out of you. The sounds and behavior are important. Let it wash over you rather than seeking the logic of what the words mean.

An Organic Experience of Letting Changes Affect You

My teacher Mr. Modica and I took the repetition work past what Meisner created it to be. It was originally created as a drill. I have watched old videos of Sanford Meisner and thought the repetitions there were not as connected as the work Modica passed down to me. It is more academic in a way that it almost doesn't have any emotional change.

In the repetition I teach, the underlying emotion can change so much. Raw behavior and pure emotional life start to emerge right away when not working off logic, but listening and going off what you're hearing. Ultimately, how it comes out of your partner affects your next repetition.

The way I teach repetition is also much more impulsive. It is more raw and reveals hidden behaviors. I use it as a guide to what you are doing, both in acting and in life. That is where you handle the mundane; perhaps they're your rules for living life.

There's a joke that the repetition exercise is great marriage counseling. If two people were about to get married and they came to me for coaching, I would teach them repetition. It takes out all the boring bits of your life and speeds up all your conflicts and joys in two minutes. It removes all the social barriers in between.

You can do the repetition exercise only with a breath. "Phew," can be an organic exchange when you work off the sound and the behavior of the breath. Within that "phew" sound, there is a lack of words that can create logic or meaning because people often want to do the exercise "right" rather than just be in the moment. When first learning the repetition exercise, I want my actors to live in it for a good month or so before adding the playwright's words or published text. Why? Because people must remove their old programming so eventually, they can play any character. I want to break preconceived outcomes or decisions actors make when playing a "character." As in my character needs to be like this or act like that. When you are playing Gypsy Rose Lee or the Cowardly Lion, you must break your idea of who and what that character is, instead, allowing the present moment to help color in the character. We have to find the world that character lives in truthfully in ourselves.

Repetition exercises are like a reality show, but without the editing. Repetition removes the trivial bits of life and gets straight to the conflict between people. You cannot back off when you get into conflicts. You have to stay in the kitchen when it gets hot. Repetition also teaches to get your attention off yourself. Once you do that, the exercise becomes spiritual. When you allow yourself to react and be in the moment, your true self starts to emerge. It also takes away the desire to look good out of the equation because you cannot do two things fully at once. (Yes, science has proven that multitasking is ineffective, and you truly cannot do two conscious, voluntary things at once.)

For example, if I am watching you nod your head. That is all that exists in the moment. If you repeat, "I'm nodding my head," how you say that starts to change how I say it. Now, it is no longer about you nodding your head. The subtext I read and then speak aloud could be, "You got upset?" Then you may reply, "Yeah, I got upset." "You got upset when you shook your head." Now, something new occurred. You notice it through repetition, and you speak about it truthfully in the moment.

Sometimes this exercise can be a problem because actors might want to search for changes because they want to do the exercise right. But it's in those moments of wanting to be right or look good that you bring yourself back to the moment to have an organic experience of letting the changes create themselves. As a teacher, I want the exercise to lead the actor, especially if it doesn't make sense to them. Sooner than later, the student's passion starts coming out in their work and what they have to say as an artist. You'll often find your artist's statement in highly emotional places where you feel you need to stop and can't go further or during a breakdown. If you are thinking, "I don't want people to see me. I don't have it all together, and I'm not confident or great," that's when you need to lean in harder to what that character and what that moment is about. At times, people experience this in their acting class and are not willing to "go there" yet. But this is where the good and gritty work lies. You must do this in your acting class, so your body has muscle memory that it can do the same in front of strangers with strangers.

I took Meisner's repetition exercise and worked it in a bit to reveal who you are in the world. From this point, the next exercise in learning to be truthful in the moment under imaginary circumstances will be creating a Personal Monologue (which we'll discuss in the next chapter). Meisner only intended to create a momentary exercise of impulse and spontaneity and then replace it with the playwright's words. Our interpretations of the exercise match up, but my version has practical applications for life as well.

PERSONAL MONOLOGUE EXERCISES

"Tell all of your story with your whole heart."

- Brené Brown

After the repetition exercise, I have my students create personal monologue number one or PM1. The prompt for the PM1 is to write out an event in your life in which you have some perspective and some distance. It also has to be difficult to talk about—you wouldn't speak about this to just anyone. Even though this PM1 event happened in the past, it is now an imaginary circumstance because it's written how you remember it and is not actually happening right now. The PM1 is entirely my creation and an exercise in writing, memorization, and performing.

Through PMs—extremely personal stories that trigger emotional responses—the actor gets the training of playing a character born from their true self. In this process, actors develop a point of view. They know exactly what every line means to them.

When actors move on from PMs to scenes, the playwright's words will have meaning to them. They will remember to bring out their point of view in response to the playwright's words.

In classes at MCS, everybody writes their own PM1, and they have one week to memorize it.

For students who come to class twice a week, they do it in their third class. I ask people to be vulnerable right away. Some people never make it to the PM1. They leave class the day it is due because they have a meltdown and create excuses as to why they can't do it. Sometimes the catharsis the exercise brings scares people away, and I never see them again. By not doing the exercise, they are avoiding the truth. But on the other hand, some people nail it, play a big game, and are hungry to do the work.

Classes are ongoing; successful long-time students stay, and new students come on board. The PM1 each person picks depends on the environment of the class. As a group, they will guide each other to a vulnerable place, ripe for a breakthrough. Class itself creates the space for the new actors to take a risk in their PM2 (more on that a little later) and really go there. Because they realize they cannot bluff in my class. They need to get to that hard-to-reach spot, otherwise, the class is not for them. I build trust by having people do what intimidates them. That is how we grow, staying in the fear and learning how to be in the unknown. And not go back to our past habits.

Sometimes I'll have students do their PM1 on the fly if they don't have it memorized, instead of reading it off the page. I might even throw them a curveball with a provocative question prompt, one of my favorites being, "What are twelve things you're afraid to say out loud?"

Responses to that can range from "I'm bisexual" to "I need to write a play about my mother, and I don't want her to know."

I find that interesting. My students often share that, "I've never even known I needed to say that." But being forced to say speak up brings out the subconscious and gives it a voice. That is what my real goal is through this exercise: to get you to work on instinct and impulse, moving you away from the automatic, the involuntary, and the ego. We often have a neatly curated way of telling the story about surviving life, but I want to get you out of that, get to the grit, and get to the true you.

We don't see that version of ourselves in the mirror. It is rare to see people who are feeling intense emotions and doing something healthy about them.

Growing or Giving Up

Your PM1 has to be written by you and memorized. And I want you to memorize the words like someone famous wrote them. You also have to detach your emotions from it and learn the words by rote (memorizing without adding pre-planned emotion or inflection in the voice). This reveals a lot to me as a teacher.

- Can you get an assignment in on time?
- Are you going to have a breakdown about it?
- Will you memorize the words you wrote, or are you going to rely on your memory of what happened?
- Are you going to let the text flow through you so you can start playing the character's point of view?

As you start your PM1, you often don't realize how important or meaningful the event you chose actually is. There's something thematically about the event that makes you have to confront a part of you that's been divided or separated out. And now, you have to include it in your acting work to move forward in my class.

After working on the script and some of the emotional triggers in the first review of your PM1, I make you act it out in your next two classes. It can be a little constricting and then healing while others grasp the exercise almost right away.

PM1 topics often, but don't always, include stuff about sexual abuse, rape, trust being broken, eating disorders, body shaming, addiction, shame, families being destroyed, breakups, abortions, familial neglect, and hopelessness.

It's such an important exercise, and it changes people's lives. Again, you have to have some distance from the event—it can't have happened last week. And it has to be true.

Sometimes I have students who are very general about their PM1. So, they have to go back and rewrite it. It was Stanislavsky who said generality is the enemy of all art, and those words ring true in my class as well.

When people are truly vulnerable during their PM1, that's when the real work begins. All I want is for you to be able to live truthfully under imaginary circumstances and to be emotionally free. It's not easy, but it's doable. You have to persevere through whatever residual pain is left within you and work with it. My students know they're in a safe place when they enter my class. But you have to stick with it because you're going to either grow or give up.

Everybody in my class grows. We all have instincts and impulses, and when you listen to them, they'll help you get out of your way. We all have truths that we don't act upon. We're all more relatable when we become vulnerable. It doesn't matter who you are. You have inner truth. We all do.

Personal Monologue 2 (PM2)

The PM2 involves writing about what blocks you. Ironically, what blocks the student sometimes keeps them from finishing the PM2.

My students don't do their PM2 until a year into their Meisner work. I won't give them a due date, but I will coach them in each class on it. I had one student tell me, "I wrote seven pages, and I still can't finish it."

I still look at it anyway. I often see what they've written down are symptoms of why or how the student got blocked. But those symptoms are not actually what blocks them. The block is a self-limiting belief they don't recognize as a block but a "truth" (albeit a false truth). They will defend this and try to prove the validity of that belief.

I'll then ask why they can't finish their PM2. Or why it feels undone or why they can't memorize the words. Often, the answer involves the self-limiting belief or the idea that the PM2 sounds stupid or isn't as good as someone else's. I can't help but smile at this and offer an answer somewhere along the lines of, "You think what you do isn't special or good enough, and you don't trust yourself. Write about that."

They then scrap their PM2 and redo it from this place. I love coaching the actor to be able to see what they had previously been blinded to. That "aha" moment is so powerful to me as a coach. I want to coach as many actors as possible into transformation and possibilities—that is my purpose in life. As a result, they can bring that freedom to their acting and in their life. Reminding audiences and those closest to them of what is possible when you get out of the narrative of self-limiting beliefs.

More PMs Come in Different Sizes

The PM3 involves writing a song. The PM4 is a love letter to yourself. The PM5 is a letter from yourself forty years from now to your younger self. The PM Credo is like writing a bunch of credos that you believe—*it's too late for me, earning money is really hard, artists can't be rich,* and so on. Then you write about how that myth somehow became real. It can get a little scary. And then there is the PM10 Commandments—"rules" the actor lives by. "Thou shall not…"

I have a PM where the actor personifies the demon in their mind. For example, I have a demon named Lola. Lola chain-smokes, is a New York agent type with a heavy New York accent, always knows better, is intolerant and impatient, and has no grace for me to grow. She always tells me, "Matt, you are not cool enough. You need me. Without me, you will be so sad and lonely. I have taken care of you since those kids deserted you in seventh grade…you don't want to be hurt again." This PM exercise is based on the idea that we all have a demon who seems likable and great at first, but then they sabotage you and embroil you in a codependent relationship.

I'll have my students write a PM Biography, where they write about a famous person and then perform it. Some of it may be true, but it doesn't have to be all historically accurate. I've had students do Janis Joplin, Whitney Houston, and Dolly Parton, among others. You can even dress like them and pick up some of their physical characteristics. It doesn't have to be gender-specific either.

REAL-LIFE EXAMPLES OF PERSONAL MONOLOGUES

"The Locker" A PM1 By Chris Russell

WHEN I WAS IN HIGH SCHOOL, I was the central figure in a nasty rumor. Someone said that the dean caught me jerking off in the bathroom. It wasn't true. It was just one of those dumb things that caught on. I actually watched that malicious grapevine begin to sprout at lunch one day. Holding my lunch tray in the cafeteria, I could see and hear each table of cliques learning of my faux disgrace, followed by them turning and laughing at me. I'd had my fair share of bullying before that, but that rumor put it on another level. Everywhere I walked in the hallway, every classroom I entered, no matter where I went, I was greeted with "Chris Russell got caught jerking off in the bathroom!" This evolved into "Russell my dick, asshole." (Russell as in rustle; maybe because one of my bullies was an aspiring English major.) That was my new nickname: "Russell my dick, asshole!"

I even went into the Staten Island AOL chat room with kids from other schools, and they knew about it. It was brutal. I couldn't even pee at school anymore because I didn't want people to see me leave the bathroom. It got so bad that I begged my parents to take me out of school. When you're fifteen, you don't understand that things like that are fleeting. I thought it would be something that would haunt me forever. Like at thirty-five, I would go to a job interview and the person looking at my resumé would say, "Hey, Chris Russell," followed by a long, drawn-out hand masturbation gesture. My parents told me to tough it out, that eventually, it would cool down. But it didn't. It went on for months.

A little later in the school year, I was in the locker room before gym class, and all the kids were giving me hell. This kid, Jimmy Bugle, started getting changed next to me. He was the smallest kid in our grade, and he was also a little slow. Totally harmless. All the bullies left him alone. And I guess he was just trying to fall in line with everyone else, but he picked up a dirty T-shirt and said, "Here, I found your jizz rag."

The locker room exploded. Everyone started laughing like hyenas. I felt my neck get hot and my heart racing. One kid screamed, "Even Bugle is herbing this kid."

There were at least three kids in that room that deserved a fucking beating from me, but I never had the balls to stand up to any of them. I don't know what I was thinking or what came over me. Maybe I was trying to make an example. Maybe I thought if I did something drastic, it would scare people into not fucking with me anymore. So, I grabbed Jimmy by the shirt—he was half my fucking size—and threw him in an empty locker, then shut it. It was one of those old ones with the combination dial on it.

I heard it click. The whole room went silent, except for Jimmy, who started pounding and screaming and crying from inside. I can still hear him now—piercing, blood-curdling screams, begging and pleading to let him out. I didn't know what to do. I panicked. I tried putting random numbers into the lock. Someone ran and got a teacher, who had a janitor pry it open with a crowbar. They pulled Jimmy out, and he was sweating and crying and hyperventilating. It looked like a giant crushed him in its hand. They had to have the nurse come in and talk him down. He was completely inconsolable.

I'd never felt so horrible in my life. I combated bullying by bullying a kid half my size. And for what? It didn't fix a thing. If anything, it made the other kids respect me less. I had girls come up to me after asking, "How could you do that to Jimmy Bugle? What the fuck is wrong with you?"

I saw him in the halls a couple of times after that, and he always walked the other way. He was fucking terrified of me.

The school year mercifully ended, and eventually, new rumors and gossip put mine in the past. Jimmy changed schools the next year. I never saw him again. And I never got to apologize.

Emotionally Inside the Locker

As a coach, my responsibility is to create an environment that people can walk into and show up without disguise. Actors and artists need to face scary things to make breakthroughs. Think of it as writing a story you'd be sorry to take to your grave.

In MCS classes, students get to do that work three times through their PM1. Most PM1s are quite profound and accidentally remarkable. A lot of them are about abuse, addiction, or secrets they kept or were made to keep since they were kids—they're moments that formed who they are. Some are accidentally funny, and some are horrible. The possibilities are endless. But they are all real stories from real people. And you would never know by just looking at the person.

After hearing Chris Russell's story, I said to him, "Emotionally and artistically, you're still in that locker."

And that moment changed everything for him. The PM1 often reveals where your creativity stopped. It is also a revelation to me, as the coach, that this is why they are in my acting class. They have something to say, but somehow, subconsciously, they got stuck. I think of my job as using the arts to retrain people to be more human because life trains you to be the opposite. The PM1 becomes the emotional preparation work, so the actor can live truthfully in imaginary circumstances no matter whose words they're speaking—the playwright's, their PM1, or their own in their daily life.

"Dear Voice"
A PM2 By Rachel Policar

Dear Voice,

Here are some things that people say about you, to me.

You're gorgeous. You give me goosebumps. You're incredible. You're flawless. You make me cry. Never heard a voice like you before. Wow, you can do anything.

Here are my responses that I say inside my head when people say these things about you, to me.

You're wrong. My voice is a train wreck. If only you knew how fucked up it really was, how broken—you'd understand that it is all a lie. I barely know how to use it. It doesn't work. My voice can't do what you think it can do. I can't sing as high as I used to, as high as other people. I'll never be able to. You just don't know what you're talking about. You only think it's good because you're too stupid to know better, because you aren't educated enough to know better. If you had educated ears, you'd hear what it really was.

Fuck. I'm sorry, dude.

I don't know, guess I got used to disappointment—to being disappointing. It always started the same, "If you get your shit together, you could really be somebody." But then things always fell apart and it became, "You are wasting your time. You're wasting your money."

I'm not accustomed to hearing or accepting when teachers tell me that I can achieve great things. I figured my ship had sailed and that I had missed the window of youth to get where I used to dream of going. And yet, I'm still showing up to classes, questing after the "right" teachers, questing after the technique. Why, if I don't believe?

I have to get it right. I can't even try unless I know that it's going to be 100% correct, 100% of the time. I need to know all the rules, all the steps. I need to know it will be perfect on the other side. I know that if I go slow and go step by step that I will ultimately get there faster—but it feels like a failure to have to go slow, to have to focus on one small thing at a time. I guess I am deeply terrified of failure.

I don't believe people when they tell me that I can do this, that I can dream big, achieve bigger. I don't believe them. Why don't I believe them? Am I afraid of success? Am I afraid of getting the opportunity to succeed and then ultimately failing? I guess I am deeply afraid of being disappointing. I have disappointed so many people in the past, and I am crippled the by the fear that I will disappoint the next person. Especially the next person who takes a risk on me, takes a chance on me, believes in me.

I fundamentally understand that ultimately, success is up to me. I have to put in the work. The "artist" part is not what needs work. I understand the shit that you can't teach. The intangibles. They are there. But I have to put in the work. If a door is opened for me and I can't walk through it and be excellent, then I will disappoint whoever opened that door. I'll feel guilt and shame and anger toward an innocent party, you, my voice, that is just trying to do the best it can—if I don't give you the tools you need to succeed, how can I expect you to come through for me when I need you the most?

What if I put in the work and I'm it's still not enough? What if I'm just kidding myself and everyone is just simply blowing smoke up my ass because no one wants to be the one to tell me to just fucking give it up, do real estate full time and have babies because devoting any more time and energy to my career is a waste of life?

I'm always looking for something to blame. If I do achieve the big things—notice I said IF because I can't even bring myself to say when—if I do achieve the big things, my dad's not going to be around to see it. Whose fault is that—my dad's? Cancer? I was mishandled for a lot of years, I tried SO hard to get the tools I needed and never did. So, is that my fault? Or is the fault of my teachers? Did they give me the tools and I just didn't put in the work? Ultimately, I'll decide it's my fault because I have to blame SOMEbody.

Now, people are giving me the tools. I'm finally getting the feedback that the tools are working. So I guess I have to keep showing up, keep diving in head fucking first, keep taking a blind leap of faith and trusting. Trusting that someone else sees in me what I've never been able to see in myself - trusting that the things people say about you might actually be true. What if they are true? What if I achieve the big dreams? What can my life look like then?

INDEPENDENT ACTIVITIES

"Hold your breath. Make a wish. Count to three. Come with me and you'll be in a world of pure imagination."

- Willy Wonka, "Pure Imagination"

TO START TRAINING THE ACTOR to live in imaginary circumstances, we must get into the world of independent activities. This is something that needs to be done independently from another person.

Part of the purpose of independent activities is to introduce emotional preparation. Independent activities incorporate the full definition of acting (living and behaving truthfully and fully under imaginary circumstances)—essentially the actor is creating mini-plays with objective emotional prep, relationship, and working off their partner. These activities are bound by two rules, and the possibilities are endless. They have to be difficult for the student to do, and there must be a compelling reason (that contains some imaginary circumstances) for doing them. For example, it could be a challenging puzzle. It could also be taking an old pair of sneakers, putting paint on them, and cleaning them thoroughly. As long as you have a reason why. You come to the class with a broken mug you got from the 99-cent store. You broke it because, in an imaginary circumstance, you had a fight with your mom. And now, you have to repair it because it's your grandmother's favorite mug. Your grandmother, supposedly, is dying. You want to bring the mug to her and put it in her casket when she finally passes. You have to fight for your objective and create that world.

The difficulty lies in concentration and in how compelling the situation is that you created. The independent activities are where students start training their imagination. The three key focuses are: focus on the thing itself, work off your partner, and get the attention off yourself (or will it off yourself). It is not about you; it is about the other person. You want to work off of them, letting them affect you while living in your new truth. Your new truth then becomes a new truth to your partner. Through back-and-forth reciprocity, things start to change. And that is how you create imaginary circumstances.

Here is one of my favorite scenarios to practice with: somebody is doing something for their dead father, who they took care of when he was sick. The actor/student was never Dad's favorite, but they sacrificed their life for Dad. Then the other sibling, who was the favorite, partied and never showed up. The father left everything to the favorite child, even though the other one took care of him.

Those things happen to people in real life. And I am training my students to react, not how you would in real life, but on instinct. They have to repeat and do an activity and work off the character who comes in with new information. I give a fake will that they open in the scene, which reveals the favorite child who did nothing gets the entire estate. I also build up the stakes (that the student/actor needs money, for example).

Through those activities, you gain superpowers. What I am really doing is training actors to explore their creative potential through the creation of hard-to-handle imaginary circumstances.

Another independent activity created in my class has involved students writing horrible words they feel about themselves over their body in marker and then trying to wash them off. Many people have found out-of-the-box ways to do extremely difficult and cool things at MCS.

The difficulty in the independent activity cannot be a theory, nor should it be intellectual. Less effective activities are realistic ones like counting receipts or doing taxes. That is too much like real life, which leaves little room for imaginary circumstances. You want to start building a world in which you get to play, and anything in close proximity to your real-life hinders you from letting go and playing. The activity needs to be difficult to do because it allows you to get your attention off yourself. And the more specific the details of the activity, the better for you to do. This specificity, for example, needs to be down to your favorite icing, which is written in a certain type of calligraphy you learned while in college. So, reproducing that calligraphy is going to create conflict and drama, and actors need to be trained in conflict and drama.

Another example. I had a student go to a gift shop in New York and buy an I Love New York mug. I asked them to break it before class, putting all the broken pieces in a paper bag. In class, I instructed them to Krazy-Glue the mug back together perfectly. The conflict in this activity is that there is a standard of perfection—an exact way the mug has to be put back together so it looks like the original.

The harder the standard of perfection in the activity, the more useful it is to the actor. You also have to give yourself a reason why that mug broke and why you need to fix it. (Remember, we need to create imaginary circumstances.) It could be that the mug is your mom's favorite, and you broke it because you got into an argument with her. Whatever the case may be, the actor needs to really take part in the activity. Not just pretend they are doing it. Participating in the action allows for real moments and circumstances to come up. The actor could have cut their finger and dropped the pieces while engaging in repetition with their scene partner. Anything can happen.

I will then suggest changing some of the circumstances. What if you got in a fight with your mom but knocked over the mug accidentally? And now you have to fix it because it's an heirloom. And to top it off, your mom is now in the hospital, and she's dying. Suddenly, a whole lot of emotional subtext starts coming out.

And the actor's scene partner is trying to work off of them while they're reconciling fixing an heirloom mug and a dying mother. And at this point, the actors are not thinking about repetition anymore. They are not thinking about doing the scene either because they are so involved in fixing this mug. Fixing the mug is a tangible thing, and while doing so, the actors are acting and reacting truthfully—which is what we want.

Find Campbell Island

Before having my students do their first independent activity, I hand them a globe of the world. I then instruct them to, "Find Campbell Island."

The goal of the task is simply to find Campbell Island (yes, it is a real place near Australia) on the globe. While one person is concentrating on finding the globe, the other person is instructed to put their attention on their partner. Meanwhile, they engage in the repetition exercise with each other. This activity gives rise to a scenario of conflict: the actor needs to divide their attention between finding Campbell Island and repeating their partner.

Three Distinct Human Knocks

The knock at the door exercise is a first-moment exercise. The person who comes to the door needs to surprise you somehow. This could be your ex-boyfriend who gave you herpes, and you haven't seen him since. It could be your adopted brother or your biological brother who you never met. Sometimes I'll give the person the opposite of what they expect—a true surprise. My goal is to trick a person's mind so they can't anticipate what is going to happen—I want them to know how to react truthfully in the unknown and in the moment. We have learned in real life not to let people see us in the unknown, so my job is to train humans to be more human.

Imagine the following MCS class scenario:

You're in your apartment. You have nothing to do. But you need to accept there are going to be three knocks at the door. Knocks have behavior behind them, and that will be the first moment in this exercise.

I then tell one of your classmates to go out in the hall and give, "three distinct human knocks with a slight space between them."

I won't intervene during the exercise. I will only side coach you. I simply want you to accept that you are going to get three knocks at your door. I want you to describe the first two knocks to me, your coach. It could be a fast knock. Or a strange knock. It is up to you what adjective you want to use. But you should not say, "it's a normal knock." There is no such thing as a normal knock. That is a made-up concept influenced by our social norms.

If you, the person on stage, respond with, "Does somebody want to come in?" I won't accept that. That is explaining or drawing a conclusion from that knock rather than describing it. At this point, you're only describing the knock.

I'll then ask, "Why are you inviting them in?"

"Because it's awkward standing here."

Then you need to say, "It's awkward standing here."

This exercise is all about working off your partner without the social obligations of real life, being courteous, kind, and whatever your opinion is on having a stranger knock on your door. You're working to be truthful in every moment with this person.

For the third and final knock, I, as the coach, don't want you to describe it to me. Open the door and express your feeling about the knock to the person in the doorway through repetition. We will see what happens.

Sometimes, I make the person slam the door on their partner. And that person in the hall has to react.

Other times, I tell the person inside not to answer the knocks at the door. The person in the hall then gets mad. And I want to see if they use that opportunity or not. I ask the actor why they didn't try to just burst in and confront their partner who left them in the hall.

Often, the actor will reply, "Because I didn't think it was part of the rules."

But it would have been the truth. Here, you need to remind yourself again of the definition of acting, which is "living and behaving truthfully and fully under imaginary circumstances." Give yourself over to the truth even if it breaks the exercise or the scene. That is how you do Meisner work as an actor.

Using What You Have and What You Want

A Meisner program generally takes two years, much like a standard academic term that most schools (and my acting teacher contemporaries) offer. It is almost an intellectual approach to an organic system that is *supposed* to break the rules, except they establish all these rules around it. They put you in a scholastic version of being an artist, which, in my opinion, does not quite work. You need structure, and you need technique. So, the Meisner work at MCS is a bit more old-school. It is slightly controversial in the way it breaks academic rules. I want to shock your body into trusting your instincts. I coach you to slap walls, stomp, jump, run, and do things out of order to retrain and rework the brain's patterns that are holding you back. The class scene work looks pretty wild, but it feels safe. It is done in a way that makes students trust me and want to show up even on days they don't want to come to class. Even when they feel a bit scared or like they want to throw up, there is still safety.

Since MCS is not broken down into a two-year program, I have actors that study with me for years or come back in between gigs and contracts. Through the years of teaching and developing, I had to ask myself how I keep the work interesting and vital while continuing to help the actor grow. What am I supposed to do with students who have been with me for three years? I had to do a lot of pedagogical thinking. I decided I would create or tailor-make new exercises based on the actor, some of which make their way into my mainstream class. One of those exercises is a specific kind of prompt—lists of fifteen things you love, hate, that trigger you, that make you want to scream, and so on. Anything to help the actor stay in their truth, get out of their head, and continuously remain authentic.

Nicole D'Angelo is an actor who came to me at the start of the pandemic. She joined two Zoom classes a week during the entirety of the pandemic. Eventually, she was so hungry for this work she moved to my in-person classes. Nicole is an Autistic actor, multi-instrumentalist, disabled advocate with a passion for theatre and musical theatre. She is also an asexual, queer-identifying, and non-binary person who uses she/they pronouns. She does not fit any box. As such, at the beginning of our work together, I decided to develop her own class just with me. We worked together on weekly prompts each week—fifteen things you love, hate, and so on. We had to try hard to find her triggers because her brain did not want her to spiral out in PTSD from a past relationship. We had to find a way to trick her brain into true emotional behavior without her shutting down or reliving it.

When I asked her to name several things that make her skin crawl, she gave answers including, Velcro, penises, and elevators. So, there does not need to be any kind of academic workbook for this work. Even the answers she gave are an option for future acting prompts.

Provocative Questions

The Provocative Questions activity is a three-step exercise. Before one initiates any form of interaction—including eye contact—with their partner, this person needs to think of a question that they know would trigger responses from their partner. Provocative questions observed in MCS classes vary from being nice to being naughty, but they cannot be filtered—meaning questions that are often used in small talk or other social occasions and are free from causing a reaction in the partner. Questions regarding family members, childhood, and one's love life are common topics up for grabs. We want those questions that sting and cause an "ouch" in their partner. Some partners may even find an age-friendly question less desirable because the other person may be assuming that they cannot handle a difficult question. However, regardless of how provocative the question is, the person being asked cannot answer the question. They can only repeat the same question. Even though the words haven't changed, the subtext of the repeated question becomes so rich. Because now it is imbued with the partner's instinctual reaction to this question.

Here is how it starts: one actor closes their eyes or bows their head, going into their imagination to come up with a question that will trigger their partner. Again, it's about the "pinch and the ouch." There are so many ways you can say the same thing. In this acting exercise, the triggering question is the "pinch," and the answer is the "ouch."

How you say "ouch" depends on the pinch. If it's a lion's-roar of a pinch, you respond with a raised tone, "Ouch." It depends on what's instigated within you and how you react. This exercise is a microcosm of what acting is: pinching, ouching, and responding.

The topics for provocative questions can range from God to sex to anything you think will make the other person react.

Step 1 is forming the question.

Step 2 is fully putting your attention on your partner and then asking the question.

Step 3 is the partner repeating your question. The two of you then go back and forth, much like in the repetition exercise.

Within Step 3, you're also describing your partner's behavior and what the question did to them. "That question made you sad." "Yeah, that question made me sad."

Provocative questions reveal the emotional life and even baggage living within the actor. That's what we want to activate. Because your brain has a polite version of the answer to a question like how you feel about your mom. But in this exercise, you get to reveal your true feelings—it could take you to a heavy place.

Allow things to take you into your inner life rather than the neat, pretty, and outward-facing parts of life. You want to activate behavior spontaneously in your partner. If you get them to repeat it, the question will take them out of their head—a place where they think and analyze the situation. We don't want logic. We don't want social appropriateness. We want this to trigger the gritty and impulsive.

Your imagination always needs to be exercised. This allows spontaneity. Everybody has an actor in them. To get to the actor in you, you have to let go of control and allow things to take you into your inner life, then allow it to come out and express itself. That is the actor in you.

Not everybody wants to let go of that control. Not everybody wants to let things affect them and be in the moment. That is the game. I train you to be open to anything. So, when the playwright gives you specific words, when you have to be on a film set, or when you have an audition, your body can act on impulse. This is why we need technique. There is a way out of your head through acting techniques. There is a way to be vulnerable and connected, using all your shameful stuff by putting it into your art and your life. That's my mission. That's what this work did for me. And that's what I'm now doing in my real life.

The world of provocative questions is also great emotional prep. Before you do a scene, a provocative question can stir something up to get you to the emotional place you need to be in for that scene. Provocative questions are great for audition technique, which we will get to in an upcoming chapter.

COLD READINGS

"The Process of becoming unstuck requires tremendous bravery, because basically we are changing our way of perceiving reality."

- Pema Chödrön, Tibetan Buddhist nun

Let It Go

A MORE ADVANCED INDEPENDENT activity I give my students is a lyric-reading exercise inspired by Modica's war-poetry-reading. The key component of this exercise is to get the words off the page, break away from logic, and find out what they mean to you. You express the lyrics to another person with your behavior. You can only read one word at a time, allowing each word to transform what's happening inside you.

I once made one of my students stand against a brick wall on 36th Street while another student stood as if they were center stage in a spotlight. I gave them lyrics from "Let It Go," from the animated film *Frozen*.

Sometimes I'll create lyric-readings using Miley Cyrus' lyrics or P!nk's lyrics. P!nk has a song called "Conversations with My 13 Year Old Self." Her lyrics are so good for Meisner because she basically writes personal monologues. I use anything and everything to get actors to cry, connect, laugh, and just be silly. I'll use the lyrics, "You came in like a wrecking ball." Or "Landslide" by Fleetwood Mac, where you need to deliver your meaning behind, "I took my love, and I took it down. I climbed a mountain and I turned around."

Whenever I ask them to repeat the words, the meaning of the lyric goes deeper in the actor, and they start letting go of the logic of the words. And as soon as they let go of the logic, something magical starts to happen. The words begin to uncover the actor's inner life. The truth comes out, and the truth will always set you free. If I'm coaching an actor on "Let It Go," and they play the lyric logically because their brain is telling them to do so, I'll let them know. Take a breath. Then lean into what's happening inside you and let that truth come out of you.

Sometimes you don't know where the breath or the moment is going to take you. You might not know where Miley Cyrus's "Party in the USA" lyrics are going to take you. You have to let those lyrics wash over you and live inside you, figuring out what they mean to you and not speaking them how you think they're "supposed to be." There is great meaning in everything in life—the pop lyric, the pain you experienced as a child, and the present moment.

When I ask actors to use pop culture lyrics as an exercise, I am asking them to let go of wanting to be poised, proper, and perfect. It is predictable, uninteresting, and disconnected from reality. Both the audience and the actor will become bored. That's why pretty people can't just rely on their looks on camera or onstage. Beauty alone is not enough to tell a truthful story. You have to be present, and you have to go deeper and be vulnerable. The heart always wins. Passion always wins. Even if you lose according to life's standards, your ability to be self-aware and connected to yourself is a win. It's in that place where one finds happiness—from the inside, not the outside like society would have you believe.

Life is not just happening to us; it's happening *for* us. I get to use what happens in life and build from it, not deny it. It's just like in repetition—every moment is changing, and it's offering you an opportunity. It's up to you, to us, to do something with that new moment. Refusing to not work with and live in the current moment—the only truth—is what causes a lot of misery.

For the purposes of acting and our work, the more attention you have on your partner, in the ever-changing moment, and the more you listen and work off them, the more truthful behavior will come out of you.

You have to let those lyrics or poems hit you. I use poetry all the time during this exercise—heightened language that will stir your emotional inner life.

I will even ask my students to use a political song or speech in a similar manner, especially when social justice and unrest are at the forefront of the news of the day. I may ask that they use "Imagine" by John Lennon, Malcolm X's "Ballot or the Bullet" speech, or Dr. King's "I Have a Dream" speech. The actor is to then recite the speech or song, line by line, stirring up emotions within them and letting them out truthfully in the moment. It helps the actor develop technique, and it helps the person wrap their head around social injustice so they can help make positive change in the world and not ignore it.

When working with an actor on lyrics or a poem for the first time, after they've recited it once, I'll stop them ask what the line means to them. And I might get an answer along the lines of, "I don't know. This character is really lonely and sad." And if that's the case, I'll ask, "How does it feel for you when you're lonely and sad? Show us that." Usually, the actor wants to recite the lyric as they think it's supposed to look and feel. But asking how they feel as the character—a lightbulb goes off in an "aha" moment. They realize that whatever they do with the lyrics, it's okay to be ugly and messy and unplanned.

I get actors sometimes who resist, who want everything to be planned and to be nice and neat. But that has nothing to do with being truthful in the moment, nor does it have anything to do with being an artist. Art is messy sometimes, and so is living in the moment. You have to learn what and where emotions live within you. You have to get out of your own way. How? You have to be coached to navigate around your blind spots and the things you can't see.

Every now and then, I have newer students who will say, "I'll do this lyric-reading exercise your way, Matt. But I need to know what's going to happen to me first." That is not going to cut it. If you only play a game where you know the outcome, that's not a game. For well-trained actors, acting is familiar, but they know the general rules or what to expect. After a lot of training, the same applies to repetition and all Meisner techniques. But I want actors to work from the unknown. To be able to work from, "Fire, aim, ready," as opposed to "Ready, aim, fire." I want you to fire first just like I want you to perform a rough draft of your PM before it's even done. It's okay if it's a mess at first. We're all about polishing and perfecting at MCS. But it's a process. First, let's get you out of your head so you can start creating action and attraction.

Secrets to Become More Attractive

After the lyric-reading exercise, I have actors do the same thing with monologues. You have to accept that the words you're speaking are your words. This exercise is a cold-reading exercise. I don't want you to have it figured out. You can't know what you're doing.

Do you know how hard it is for us to show people that we don't know what we're doing? Do you know how attractive people are who can admit fault or take accountability?

Take something small, like tripping in public. People often try to act like they didn't trip. Or they bring a lot of attention to themselves, rather than acknowledging what happened and then moving along. Why pretend or deny or overdramatize the situation? It's because of the ego. But denying the ego and putting it away makes for a much more attractive person.

What makes me a great teacher and MCS special is love. When someone loves the good, the bad, and the ugly about you, they feel accepted, seen, and heard. We were raised with the idea that we shouldn't be vulnerable and that we need to have it all together. Never let them see you sweat. But acting training is different. It's about—can I see you struggle? Can you put that struggle into the character? Because the characters you play are people who feel just like you. It's okay to be frustrated when the playwright's words aren't resonating with you or if you're having a block in the moment. Use it. It's infinitely more attractive to mess up a little rather than having some idea of perfection play out coldly and methodically.

EMOTIONAL PREP

"One important key to success is self-confidence. An important key to self-confidence is preparation."

- Arthur Ashe, professional tennis player

EMOTIONAL PREP IS LIKE warming up the car before you drive. Let's say that, at first, my dad was happy I wrote a book. Then I wrote a chapter on him and made him upset. And then he sued me—that could be one way for me to prepare emotionally for a scene. I can imagine it, and it's horrible, but it's something that could help the inner part of me suppressing those feelings and responses to come alive during a scene.

Pain and Pleasure

If you look at TV commercials and consumerism, they are motivated by pain and pleasure. Everything is. Maybe you feel stuck in your life and your behaviors don't match your values. You have not dealt with enough of your pain to move past it but part of you is engaging in pleasurable activities to avoid having to deal with the pain. It is like having your foot on the brake and the gas at the same time.

There was once this exercise in class, where I prompted a student, one of my great assistants, Broadway actor Danielle Jordan. I began to coach Danielle, "You are taking care of everyone but you. Your career is all about caretaking and it is a way to avoid yourself. They are not your people, and you need to fire them. Say you are firing them."

She then repeated, "You are fired. You are fired." I made her do this a few times, so her body could have the feeling of being freed from the old brain pattern so a new, stronger pattern could replace it.

Helping the actor see the cost of unconscious biases and blind spots full of self-limiting beliefs is incredibly rewarding. It is a powerful moment in my classroom.

Sometimes I coach actors to the place where their old way of doing causes so much pain that they want out of it. They realize their old baggage is so heavy that they will give it up and live in the unknown of a new future. From there, you're able to build muscle so you can live in the unknown with your art and in your personal life.

Not knowing who you are and being uncomfortable in the moment are often the building blocks of self-sabotage and two major factors that keep you from success. That's why many of us don't grow or engage in quick fixes that don't work.

That is why the Meisner work is transformational: it builds new brain patterns to call you into the future, so your brain doesn't even want the old way of being. It wants the excitement and the adrenaline from the fear of the unknown. You crave the fear and the future you can't see. You know all about your old baggage and are over it—you want the new stuff. I know you are worth more than the old, self-limiting way of being—and I want you to realize it too.

How does self-sabotage manifest in class or in the work? During a scene or the repetition exercise, it might look like inappropriate giggling (inappropriate meaning incongruent with what's happening in the moment), putting hands in pockets, a prolonged sigh, no eye contact or too much eye contact, constant chatter, or even an emotional unraveling.

What's the first remedy when self-sabotage begins to rear its ugly head? I simply ask the actor to breathe. Allow what's going on inside to match the outside. Then, incredible breakthroughs start happening. You see the actor surrender, and something greater occurs—the truth builds up inside them and oozes out of every pore in their body. It is absolutely riveting to see people be in the moment.

Like Danielle, many actors fall into the role of caretaking. If we are needed, then we have value, thus giving us an identity. If you are taking care of other people, you will think you are important. And by then, you have avoided dealing with yourself. So that incident with my student Danielle reflects how she is managing everyone and her career, rather than dealing with her inside world. This leaves the caretaker in last place, and they don't even know what they want.

Actors' POV

As an actor, you have to stay open to experience your point of view. The repetition exercise starts to bring out one of the major things in acting, the actor's point of view, or POV.

You must always have a point of view on everything you are saying during the repetition exercise or lyric-reading exercise or while rehearsing a scene. This is different from how you raise a child, "you better think before you act." Acting training is "act before you think." To get good acting, you need to be in the moment and in tune with your impulses. Emotional prep work helps a great deal when figuring out your POV.

Our Minds and Emotional Prep

Our minds are meaning-making machines. To make sense of anything we see or feel, the brain assigns meaning to it; often more meaning than it actually deserves.

Your friend didn't call you back and you're upset about it. The only reality here is that someone didn't call you back. But you might perceive some other underlying meaning. So, you make up a story in your head about it. The brain has to make sense of everything to relieve the cognitive dissonance (e.g., "I'm deserving of a call back, thus the other person must be mad at me for some ridiculous reason."), so it turns the situation into a problem. Some human beings are addicted to problems. They give some people a sense of identity. For some of us, they create the attention we crave. There are a lot of things people can do with problems.

Perception and meaning create emotions, behaviors, and characters. You always manipulate what things mean to you. However, it's time to unlearn this as an actor through various exercises like the repetition exercise.

Words Have Meaning in Emotional Prep

Certain words for some people have certain meanings. Words and language motivate us. Words and language also shut us down or even cause pain. With emotional prep, you are changing your natural state into a fantasy world. One way to do this is to trigger yourself by asking yourself a provocative question. Sometimes imagining a provocative question can trigger your emotional life.

Maybe you have an old friend who loves you. From here, your brain can create a scenario where this person is obsessed with you and has a room filled with all your photos. This could be emotional prep to help you get ready for scene work with a partner. You are changing your natural state to figure out where your character is coming from. The more you know yourself, your triggers, and the things that make you want to create a story, the more you can manipulate it all to do better scene work or have better auditions.

If You Try to Make It Happen, It Won't

The tricky part about emotional prep is that you are working for a result. But if you try to make the result happen, it will not happen. The actor needs to surrender a bit. You even have to surrender to the idea that you don't want to surrender. Your brain likes to be in control at all times, and you have to give that up. Sometimes it doesn't want to embrace technique or put its attention on the other partner, repeating and taking in what you're getting from your partner, truthfully.

Acting work is like driving a car. I'm driving to Iowa. My brain knows I'm driving to Iowa. You have to deal with what happens to you on the drive. There is a skunk in the road. I missed a turn. The sun was clear in the sky for long stretches of the drive. I had an accident the police investigated it. So many things happened on my journey to Iowa. And while I'm driving, I have to be present and in the moment—the skunk, the police, the accident, the beautiful sun. I'm not in my brain. I'm driving, which is my action or objective.

But only focusing on the objective is how some people approach acting, which is anti-Meisner. Of course, one always needs an objective. The intellectual theory of acting states that a character always wants something in a scene. Duh. But you need to know how you feel about the thing you want or your objective. What does that mean to you? What does that mean to this character? Does it match? If it doesn't, you have to find a way to trigger it, so the underlying emotional life of the character and scene rings of truth. Audrey in *Little Shop of Horrors* has an objective, but her underlying emotion is shame and feeling like nobody will love her as she is.

Sanford Meisner would give an example of a cork in the river. The cork moves according to the current or a leaf in the wind. It will move it, it will get it wet, but it won't ruin it. The cork retains its physical state and goes along with the winds and the rains. It accepts it. It moves with it.

Now take an oak tree. This is how most of us come to acting or emotional prep. I want to be exactly like (fill-in-the-blank); it needs to look like (fill-in-the-blank). An oak tree is solid, it looks and acts and is a certain way, and it will not be moved. Then a hurricane comes, knocks the tree over, and kills it. The unwavering rigidity you've brought to the scene through your version of emotional prep ends up killing the scene. Instead, you want to be that cork in the river. Dangerous currents will happen. But you must accept what's going on, and you've got to work with it. By working and moving with it, you move forward moment to moment in the scene.

The Emotional Life of Disney Characters

All Disney characters have a rich inner life and go through what's called the hero's journey. They face tremendous obstacles, but they can't do it on their own. They have to be vulnerable to "win" or achieve their goal or objective. A rich inner life and going after a high-stakes goal are essential to acting. The hero (you) must be vulnerable and do something they have never done before. This calls for the character to summon a different kind of strength—one they never knew they had before. In *Beauty and the Beast*, real love, an internal sensibility that also involves self-love, is the only thing that will break the curse—it can't be faked or done externally. Harry Potter isn't about magic; it's about a young boy finding himself and becoming a well-rounded human being within that world. *Star Wars* isn't about aliens or lightsabers; it's about relationships and bringing about order both to the galaxy and the characters' inner emotional lives.

The imaginary circumstances created—the dancing candlestick, the Patronus, the Ewok family—are incredible in each story. But in each, the protagonist or protagonists have to give up something to achieve their high-stakes objective. They don't always look good going after that goal, but they lean on themselves and the team, and in the end, they're even more loved (yep, I'm even looking at you, Vader).

It's not true love, avenging my dead parents, or taking over the galaxy that makes the character happy; the "thing" they may think they're in pursuit of. It's learning how to be during the journey. For us, we often think we will be happy when we get something—such as a spouse, losing X amount of weight, and finally getting that Tony award. But things don't make us happy. It's who we're becoming while in pursuit of something bigger than ourselves. The objective isn't going to make you happy as an actor, it's the journey of being in each moment while doing it.

Exercise for Emotional Prep

After your scene is memorized (more about this in the *Spoon River* section later in the book) and you've done the emotional prep and several independent activities, it's time to insert the playwright's words. Then we can start working off each other again. It's almost an improv situation. It's still as real inside you and you're letting it come out organically, like with repetition. We're still living in imaginary circumstances, but we're using the playwright's words. And when you present the scene in class, I want it to be messy. It doesn't need to be the proper way to do the scene. I don't want the right performance for the national tour production or your Broadway debut. All I want is for it to be truthful in the context of what's happening in your body, driven by what's happening in the moment and with your scene partner. You're in an imaginary circumstance that you accept, working off your partner, your behavior affecting one another. If you're going to scream, yell, cry, or go silent, it can't be for the sake of being theatrical but rather because your reaction is a direct result of whatever your partner is giving you. Everything you do is up to your partner, just like during the repetition exercise.

For the first couple of showings of the scene, I want the actors to be loose and free. You're just letting yourself play. You want to be specific about your relationship to the other person and where you're coming from (after doing emotional prep). If the scene calls for you to enter while screaming and crying, the specificity of emotional prep will help you get to that place. Trust in your imagination to help you emotionally prepare.

Another reason I don't want actors to have their scene set is so I can coach them on it—without them trying to be professional or to "do it right" in front of the class. I want the truth. The messy, organic, and weird must be part of the process (that otherwise would be edited out).

The coolest moments in film and TV often happen unscripted. The famed director Bob Fosse would sometimes whisper dirty things in an actor's ear before they started filming, just to get a certain reaction on film. Fosse was Meisner trained, and the technical term for what he was doing is posing a provocative question.

You want that first moment in a scene to be real. If I were working with an actor who needed to come from an unhinged place to start a scene, I would first ask, "Do you trust me?" If it's a yes, then I might ask a few more questions, and I'd have them wait to start the scene. If the scene starts outside class, I might then take a glass of water, open the door, throw water on their face, slam the door, and then have them come in and start the scene from that place. At that moment, they are so alive. They do the whole scene from that uncomfortable and unhinged place. It's incredible to watch because you got them out of their head at the start. And in the next class, I'd have you start the same scene but without the water. My intention is not to make the actor mad or look bad but add an element of surprise that brings them alive.

You must give your brain permission to play, to use your imagination. Just like when we played cars and Barbies and action figures as kids. It felt real at the time. When I played hide and seek in my neighborhood growing up, I knew it was a game, but the feelings that came out of it were real. As an actor, you want the action during an exercise or scene to come out of you, just like when you played hide and seek. Own it and live in it.

More on Emotional Prep Exercises

Meisner said that no matter how much therapy you engage in, there will always be two core triggers in your life that will never be resolved. One is "will I be loved?" and the other is "am I okay?" These two triggers or their inverse (e.g., "I'm loved" and "I'm okay") are great places from which to start emotional prep before a scene.

I also like anxiousness and nervousness as emotional prep. When you are anxious, your body doesn't know the difference between that and excitement. So now, anytime I'm nervous, I just say I'm excited. It tricks me into accepting it. I stop fighting whatever is and I actually work with it. It's my emotional prep work.

I also do an exercise with a blank piece of paper and an envelope and say you got a letter in the mail. I want you to imagine getting really good news in the letter. The letter will remain blank, but you need to decide what's on it before you open it. You need to know the wording, the penmanship, and the font. Then, you need to open it in front of the class and react truthfully as if you are silently reading it.

I'll do it with the whole class. Student A gets good news—she found out she got accepted into her grad school of choice. Student B needs both good news and bad news.

Perhaps he got hired for his first Broadway show. But then he got a letter from his doctor regarding some health issues and now he has to drop out of the show. You have to create scenarios from your imagination that could trigger you while reading the note. And then you open the letter in front of the class and react to it like you would at home alone. You can't have your reaction planned. You know the scene because you memorized the words. But you don't know *how* the words are going to come out of you because you haven't worked with your scene partner yet.

This same exercise can be done with a phone call. I call this exercise Fantasy Phone Calls (and I'm not talking about the old 900 numbers). Fantasy phone calls are where you call someone you would never have an opportunity to speak to in real life. They may be way out of reach, incarcerated, or dead. And you're only allowed to say three words to them. The three words must be memorized before you come on stage. It could be "I love you" or "I forgive you." The words don't always have to have a logical order or sequence, but they must have meaning to you.

It is my job to coach actors to eliminate the masks they hide behind and the people-pleasing versions of themselves. One way to achieve this is through emotional prep work before an exercise or scene.

CHARACTER WORK

"I never think of my characters as good or evil. I play them as honestly as I can."

- Dennis Haysbert, American actor

Impediments

I CAN CERTAINLY WRITE A WHOLE book on character work. For now, we are just going to scratch the surface. Nowadays, you can find a lot of Meisner activities on Google. There is even a video where Meisner is coaching a guy with a balancing stick on his hand. He is doing it for a good reason. The balancing work is physically hard to do. Similar activities include painting your toenails without using your hands. This is what we call the world of impediments.

An impediment is a barrier to doing something. An impediment could be blindness, making actors accept that they are blind by having them do acting exercises or scene work with their eyes closed. You could have a speech impediment, or the script could call for you to be deaf. I have coached actors in plays that call for a missing limb, a broken arm, or a dysfunctional dominant hand. Back pain, stomach pain, headache, migraine, stubbed toe, or a toothache are all impediments as well.

How do you deal with an impediment and make it believable to an audience? I help actors do that through exercises.

Let's say the script says that you don't have the use of your right ear. I would ask the actor I'm coaching, "Can you accept that?" If the actor says yes, then they begin the exercise. Every time I snap my fingers in this exercise, I want you to have excruciating pain in your right ear. Throughout the exercise, I keep adding to the difficulty of the impediment being worked on.

These independent activities will eventually lead to scene work. Right now, you're using these independent activities to further enhance the technique you're building in the repetition exercises, learning to work off your partner, trusting your instincts, and getting out of your way and out of your head.

Character work is impediment work. You're still listening and working off your partner, but you're accepting and adding various physical or emotional realities. Maybe you have a massive headache in the scene. Or you're sobering up from being drunk. It could also involve a physical or learning disability. This is all character work and impediment work, where your job is to present a believable illusion to the audience.

If you have to have a hangover in a scene, the key is not how *you* would experience a hangover. It's how a hangover is viewed truthfully by an audience. So, you ask yourself, what are the characteristics of being drunk or hungover? It could be sloppy, trying not to look drunk, so maybe you slur your words. You pick up a couple of characteristics, and you make them your own. You practice character work and impediments just like practicing memorizing lines. And it becomes habitual or second nature.

REAL-LIFE CIRCUMSTANCES

"You can't stop the waves, but you can learn to surf."

- Joseph Goldstein, writer, Buddhist teacher

How do you get out of your head in the audition room? How do you conduct yourself during the audition?

Acceptance

So much of acting is about acceptance. You have to accept imaginary circumstances, the playwright's words, and/or the socio-economic world and backstory of a character. What era are they living in? What gender/s are they? What's their racial background, and does it influence how the world sees them (or not)?

You have to create the world of the character you're playing. The time period. The place. Their accent (if any). The character's upbringing. How they dress. How they walk. And more.

An audition for a TV show is going to be a little different than a theatre audition. And an audition for *Grey's Anatomy* or *Yellowstone* is going to be different from an audition for *Ted Lasso* or *Black-ish*. In part, this means that you must know what you're auditioning for and get into the world of a half-hour sitcom or a one-hour drama. These worlds are different—you have to watch some TV to get the feel of *Law & Order* vs. *Big Bang Theory*.

Auditioning is a place where you dance between your fears and dreams in one moment.

You have a limited amount of time to go in there, be yourself, make some choices, leave your work in the room, and then exit. It all goes by fast, and you have to be able to stay grounded and in the moment when your nerves start telling you to go back to your old, automatic way of behaving. Oh, and there are no props, lighting, scenery, or other actors to work off of except for a reader. You have to craft all of that with your imagination.

There's not a lot you can't control during the audition process, but you can control how you show up in the room. You can use an affirmation to help. "I'm going to show up and be vulnerable and present and open to every possibility and outcome." "I'm trained well, and I'll take whatever I get from my partner and work off of them." "I'm going to learn from this audition, no matter what."

You have to set an intention beyond whether or not you get the role or part. That kind of all-or-nothing mentality isn't helpful or healthy. It's perfectionism and being hard on oneself, and I want you to get away from that. You have value and worth and are lovable no matter what happens.

You need to accept where you are. And from there, you need to choose what you want to do and who you want to be in the audition room. And then you need to be open, and you need to connect with the people behind the desk. They're just people, and they want you to do well. They're trying to find the best people for their project. And even though they have an idea of what they're looking for, you never know until someone comes in and actually auditions.

Attitude and Atmosphere

The best things in my life are things that came about by accident. So, of course, you want to do well and book the job. But you still have to try to enjoy the journey while you're waiting to book work and focus only on what you can control. What can you control? Your attitude and how you affect every audition room you walk into.

Take your attention off yourself just like we do during the repetition exercise. Do not take anything that happens in that audition room personally, writing a false narrative in your head about people's actions or reactions. You must simply work to be present. Be professional, but allow yourself to mess up. (Casting directors like to see how an actor is able to maintain resilience.) Ask questions if you don't know what to do. A film audition is a little different from a theater audition, and both are different from a commercial audition or a voice-over audition. Ask if they want you to look at the camera. Ask if they want you to read to them or to a scene partner. You'll never know unless you ask. The people in that audition room want you to be the best you can be.

Do not worry about being a people pleaser. Your job is to interpret the text truthfully and take any direction given at face value. Often, we want to please so much in the moment that we get eager and over-correct or go too far. And then the truth of the moment and your learned technique goes out the window. You have to learn how to add to what you're doing and not subtract.

What else can you control about the audition? The emotional prep for your piece, giving yourself a first moment where you're responding to discovering the precipitating incident of the scene before you begin or before you walk in the room.

For TV shows, your agent gets the sides, and they email them to you. And then you have to work on your sides in advance. Be as familiar with the sides as possible so you don't need to look at them. Bring them with you but try your best not to use them during the audition. You want to memorize as much as possible so you can be as truthful in your action and reaction to what your scene partner is giving you or what the text is calling for. The aim is still to live truthfully in imaginary circumstances.

Language is important. Your self-talk, how you speak to yourself about yourself, needs to be healthy and kind. Because what you focus on, you create. Your self-talk can inform the way you prepare for a scene, affect the emotional prep work you do, or begin to ignite the character or the world of the text you're working on.

> "Try not to become a person of success but try to become a person of value."
>
> - Albert Einstein

You can prepare your entrance, how you enter a room and speak to the auditors. You never know who you're going to run into when you walk into the building. You must choose to show up to the audition as a person of value rather than someone who wants success and will walk over anyone to get it. Being a person of value in an audition means that you show them you're an easy person to work with. A person of value puts their ego away and tries to help others (yes, even the "competition") and does their best to stay present in every moment. A person of value creates from a place in their heart rather than a bank account, ego, or want for stardom.

You can prepare how you engage with your auditors in the room. You can practice asking about their day, or you can practice how to answer questions about yourself. If I were going to an audition, I might practice answer questions about being a teacher, Christian, gay, or how the Meisner work changed my life.

You also prepare your exit, or how you leave the room and the pleasantries you engage in with the auditors on your way out.

You can control that first moment of the scene in the audition, knowing where your character is coming from and what happened prior to the scene. When starting your piece, take a moment, and bow your head to get into the world of the scene. Sometimes you have to do something physical to get into the emotional life of the scene. It might be a posture change, a finger snap, or shifting your feet. Whatever helps you get to the place you need to be.

Depending on the world of your character, dressing the part is often a great idea. You don't have to be in full costume, but choose something that informs the time period or the character itself. Clothing can change our perspective and help us feel different emotions.

Sometimes in the audition, they may give you two different sides. Why? They handpick scenes that show the range of emotion you're capable of as an actor. If you're auditioning for Elphaba in *Wicked*, they may pick a scene where the character is vulnerable and another where the character is tough as nails.

Just like your emotional prep exercises, independent activities, and scene work in acting class, you do that work in an audition. It's just quicker and shorter. And you have to let go of the result, even though your brain wants one immediately.

Sometimes you work with a reader who won't give you much. You have to imagine what this reader could be giving you if the scene was flushed out. You get to know that telling me about catching me cheating is heartbreaking, even the reader is reading it like dead. Then, it's the actor's responsibility to craft that. Sometimes the other person reading it dead or not even looking at you in a scene of conflict sets you off. Use it. Use that as your emotional prep and get their attention, that would snap them. That is how the Meisner Technique helps you in real life.

But if you really listen to your reader, sometimes you can't work off of them because they are flat. Instead, they will start looking at you because everybody wants to be listened to. As soon as you feel like someone's listening to you, it engages you differently. That is exactly like real life—how you listen to people is powerful. It can change people.

Listening at an audition can change the energy in the room. But there are times you can't or it's incredibly difficult. Sometimes the energy in the room in an audition is bad enough. You still have to remind yourself to go with it like you would in your acting class. Sometimes you have to change the energy of the room.

As an acting coach, I'm always creating the energy of the room. If people are responding slowly to me and losing their focus, I have to change the energy of the room. I have to be mindful of their minds. You can change the energy of the room by giving people what they need without losing yourself by taking care of them emotionally. That is, by no means, easy.

Then there is a final moment. Give yourself that moment and let it settle back down into being in the room. Don't just say thank you and rush out the door. Be present. If you are in an emotional scene, let the emotions play out. If something is really funny, let it settle down before you make eye contact with the people behind the desk and say, "thank you." Be thankful that you got to do your work today. "Thank you for receiving my work today." Having gratitude that you get to be an actor and be here and show up and how amazing it is to be alive and working toward who you want to be on this planet. You are simply auditioning for it. You don't control anything else here. You think you have to show up in a certain way, have to get that call back, and have to be on a TV show. You think otherwise your life is not happy.

Tony Robbins told a story about when the first astronauts who went to the moon came back, they all became alcoholics or drug addicts, or both. They had no other life goals. There was no meaning in their life. They already achieved their wildest dreams. They had no idea how to find gratitude and appreciation. Their brains were so wired for the greatest thing in the world. Then when the greatest thing in the world happens, you have nothing else to imagine. You have no identity, and you have to recreate patterns. Tell the noise in your brain that regardless of what happens in the audition room, you are building a meaningful life. This approach will be a game-changer in your everyday life and in your art.

SCENE WORK AND SPOON RIVER ANTHOLOGY

"It ain't about how hard you hit. It's about how hard you can get hit and keep moving forward. How much you can take and keep moving forward. That's how winning is done!"

- Rocky Balboa

I'LL TAKE A SCENE FROM A Broadway play, hand my students the pages, and tell them their character's name. I have them ignore all punctuation and all fonts—italic, bold, underlined, and all caps. I tell them to ignore what the playwright or the original stage manager of the Broadway show wrote in parentheses like angrily, happily, sadly, or any other kind of emotional clue. And you'll do with these words what was done in the song lyric exercise. You're taking what the words mean to you at that moment, using them to affect your partner, and responding truthfully to what your partner is giving you while using the playwright's words.

This is a cold reading. It's also called a contact reading. I call it a cold reading that becomes warm. As you do it, your impulses start to match the writing. I've seen cold readings that are better than performances. The more alive they are, the more active, connected, and impulsive they are in the moment.

In preparation for the next class, you'll take the scene and memorize it by rote. There's no emotion attached to the words, so you're not stuck in one way of saying it. And you're not memorizing emotionally how it's going to come out of you. It's important that you're not memorizing any kind of. You want to be in the moment like in the repetition exercise, except now using the playwright's words.

Spoon River Anthology

Spoon River Anthology is a book written by Edgar Lee Masters in the early 1900s of a fictitious town in the 1800s called Spoon River. The book includes epitaphs of characters who died in the town. They are all in some way connected. Some of them are funny; some of them are horrific. The book is used a lot in high-school English and drama classes.

The text is like little monologues of dead people coming back from the dead, talking to the living. And they talk about their stories in a poetic way. Many of the stories use heightened language, and we get to see the character being developed through the text.

Sometimes, the monologues are symbolic. It doesn't spell out how they died or what happened to them, but you have to use your imagination.

I take *Spoon River* and turn it into an acting exercise for my students. I give them one of the monologues and have them memorize the words exactly. That's what Meisner would teach. And here, we get to do some character work. You might get to play a ninety-year-old woman who died from strangulation. If you come back to life, strangulation will affect how you speak, and I may even have you put makeup of the handprint on your neck. I want all of that—as close to reality as possible. I also have them perform the monologue with music playing in the background. It's almost like you're making a video. I also allow the actor to set the scene in any century. You can place it in the 1990s or the 1790s.

Character work is interesting when people have to change their voices; they find different truths in themselves to say words that they would never say because it's heightened language while placement of their voice is resonating in a different part of the head or body (e.g., speaking from the diaphragm vs. speaking from your nasal cavity). Character work is a great introduction to develop the ability to take words and allow them wash over you truthfully.

Sometimes I make people write their own Spoon River about their life—past, present, and future. It'll even cover fictional parts like how they died. I use them in a modern twist on the Meisner work. I might make them play different genders or have them write monologues for one other.

No matter what I have my students do, there's trust built into my class. In the beginning, when you're new, I'm careful who I pair you with. I'm sensitive and aware about any of my students who come from historically marginalized backgrounds. I need to provide a space where they feel safe, are allowed to be themselves, but are still challenged.

IN CLOSING

"Acknowledging the good that you already have in your life is the foundation for all abundance."

- Eckhart Tolle

Gratitude and Appreciation

AT THE END OF EVERY CLASS, I do one thing. We go across the room, and each student will name one person for whom they are grateful for that day. We don't have enough gratitude for the seemingly mundane and what we have. If you didn't get that callback, be grateful for being considered. If you don't have enough stability as an artist, be grateful for staying true to what you love. Gratitude is a significant part of being an artist, and it's important to living life. It helps provide perspective, and it is scientifically proven to temporarily boost one's mood.

What am I grateful for?

My students, the acting community that makes me whole, and my teacher Mr. Modica who inspired me to be the teacher I was born to be. I am grateful I can still do my work after more than twenty years. Doing Meisner work makes me feel important. It provides me with value. It makes me feel like I'm part of something bigger than myself, and I have something to help the world with. I'm grateful I get to coach people toward an aha moment or through a piece of some old identity that doesn't serve them anymore. I feel like I'm part of a healing process. It gets me out of my head and is the "me" that I've gotten to create as an adult.

It took me a long time to learn the Meisner work. Two of the hardest things I have done in my life were quitting smoking and learning Meisner work. To quit smoking, I had to change my belief system to create new brain patterns. "If I smoke, then I am creative." Cigarettes were associated with an old belief system of being cool, being an actor, and being artsy. Meisner work demanded me to leave myself alone and not fix myself or try to feel good. Everything I was experiencing was valid and the world would relate to these parts of me if I had enough courage not to handle them but express them through the exercises.

The Meisner work calls for you to surrender and give up attention on yourself and put it on the other person. To work through the hard days when your brain does not want you to be seen. Your shame and your innate vulnerability start to be in conflict with the act that you created to be loved as a child.

I am most proud of myself for giving back, training, coaching, and impacting other people to help them get out of their own way in art and in life. That is the greatest gift I can give. This is the legacy I am leading with and leaving this planet. It allows me to keep loving myself.

Pursuing acting led me to play my truest self—honoring every part. Ultimately, it led me to my true calling of being an acting coach, thus confirming that life is happening *for* me and not *to* me.

Finding Your Why

"He who has a why to live for can bear almost any how."

- Friedrich Nietzsche

There is no business like show business. She can be a cruel mistress and you need to be prepared for disappointment. What do you do when you question why you are still an actor? You can't control when things happen in your career or how things happen, but you can control your "why."

You must find your why. It has to move and push you through the brightest of days and darkest of nights. Interestingly enough, "how" things happen in your career will start to reveal itself a little more if your "why" is strong and specific.

How many of us focus on what we don't have or can't control and wonder why we are unhappy? Look how we have trained our brains. But we can rewire and recondition. We can figure out *what* we need and *why* we need it. That capability already lives within us. We can work from a place of *be it, do it, have it*, as opposed to what the world has taught us—have it, do it, be it. What does that mean? The world has taught us that if you want to call yourself an actor, then you can only be that by doing things like auditioning and being in plays. I say, call yourself an actor now. If you are an actor, then you will naturally start doing things indicative of that. And you'll have whatever you're looking for when you first started calling yourself an actor. What kinds of beliefs do you need to take on right now to be the type of actor you want to be in the future?

We need to raise the state and standard of how we have defined ourselves in the past. Working from a place of being it, doing it, and having it will help you add on real-life character traits you may have never known you were capable of. You start developing healthy habits aligned with the spiritual, emotional, and artistic journey we're on. And you start attracting what you want and need, coming from a place of abundance. Be proud of yourself for reading this book and for working to develop your art and your life. You're doing the best you can, and you're doing a damn fine job of it.

If You Are Stuck in Your Art or Life

Find the stuff you love and cultivate it in your life. Let it be frivolous and silly, whether it be ice skating or just riding your bike and screaming through Central Park. As Julia Cameron says, "We forget that the imagination-at-play is at the heart of all good work."

When I was a kid, I loved to play with my stuffed animals, making them come alive as different characters. Anytime I see something interesting, I think, *Can I stage that?* There are so many kinds of places that could be a theater or a stage. I still do that when I see a vacant shop in New York City. I wonder, *Could that be a new home for me and MCS?* I love theater. I love actors. I love playing in that world.

You have to find the things you love in life and let yourself play in those spaces. And then, perhaps, you can learn how to earn a living there. Society tells us something different—that you have to make money from art, or you have to make money before you get to play as an artist. But when we approach it from a monetary standpoint first, a lot of joy is lost. You don't want to fall out of love with your art. So, you have to have a healthy relationship with your dream. You have to shift it at times and grow with it. You get to be mad at it sometimes, too.

If you want to get better at acting, you have to get a coach. You need to get into an acting class, at least. Make sure it's based on instincts and impulses, and that will uncover some of your personal blocks. I've interviewed thousands of actors in more than two decades as a teacher and coach. I interview everyone, and I ask about their training. That's the first place my eyes go on a resumé. I don't care if you've had Broadway credits. It is about how you have been trained, what language you speak, or which technique you use. I also want to know what life work you have done and your mindset. What makes you a well-rounded person? Do you have a background in sports, teamwork, or dance? What kind of education do you have? What kind of work have you had to do presently or in the past? What has your life has been like to get you to this moment? How have you had to recreate yourself throughout life?

In my life and in my work, I am looking to meet great characters and ultimately become one. When it comes to actors in training, I can tell by the way they talk, whether or not their training was transformational for them. I can tell those who won't go to whatever place they need to as an actor. They struggled, looked bad in front of people, and surrendered. You need a class that is about uncovering and repairing the parts of you that have been lost and damaged so you can bring every bit of yourself to every artistic moment. Every part of you is valid and necessary. I try to help my actors create who they want to be in the world and on stage or on camera.

Define yourself as how *you* see yourself and the person *you* want to become, not what you think you should be or how you think the world sees you already. What you think, you become. So, you must retrain your brain to think healthier, better, more compassionate thoughts about yourself.

Part of my self-definition is that of an acting teacher. And I've learned so much because of the acting teacher hat I wear. I grow, but I still fall at times, and I can take responsibility when I do. Being an acting coach is a safe place for me to really be myself. It is one of the places from which my importance and value are derived. I don't always know how to carry all that over into my real life at times. Sometimes there's a real split, and I can say I'm still healing. We all have behaviors and old patterns that don't serve us. But we're all learning and growing. So, let's no longer be so hard on ourselves.

If you're a boxer, using a reference to *Rocky*, whatever you're going through in boxing is also what you're going through in your personal life. So many aspects of our experience as an actor or creative are parallel and symbolic to what's going on with us personally. You need the experience of getting it out and channeling it into your art.

You are taking an acting class, but it's actually part of a process to help you grow holistically as a person. To help integrate all parts of you in your everyday life, neglecting nothing. You have to live that way to make an impact in the arts. So, find a way to do that, either through MCS or some other person or process. I hope that this book is a supplemental support in some way. Oh, and please visit me on social media—say "hi" anytime. If you need a coach or class, you can reach out to me anytime. My handles on Instagram are: MCSTheatre and Matt.The.Acting.Coach. You can also reach me via email: matthew@matthewcorozinestudio.com.

A Few Final Thoughts

Practice this work as best you can if you can't get into a physical acting class. Get together with another friend and fellow actor. Work on things like provocative questions and the repetition exercise. React to what you're hearing or seeing from them. You can also be open and aware in life and lower the noise in your brain as much as you can. This is you removing your attention from yourself, controlling your ego, and being present.

You can only do one thing fully at a time. Do your thing, practice the art of that, work on listening, be smart, and be attracted to other people's behavior. I teach my actors to pay attention to how people act and react when no one's looking. Learn how people behave when they think no one's watching. Are they really in the moment? Or are they on? As an actor, you need to be on, but you need to be on in a way that looks and feels truthful. It's a heightened reality.

You also have to find your tribe of people while on your journey. People who you can look back with and say, "Those were the good old days, and I didn't even know it at the time." Every one of us needs to be a part of a community—it makes the journey more bearable when things get difficult and sweeter when times are good.

How do you find the balance between pain and pleasure, stagnation and growth? You need to find your tribe. You need to find people who accept you for who you are but who also challenge you to become a better artist and person. We all need to lean on somebody. A person who makes you feel good or allows you to feel your present self is in a good place. My acting class is a place of connection, safety, and dignity—but if it were a feel-good room only, no one would grow. I hope to create a "safe space for people to do unsafe things that need to be done," to quote the famous playwright John Patrick Shanley.

You can't only subscribe to the parts of life that feel good. You have to live with all of it. We learn about living a full life by being in community with others, seeing people be vulnerable, and experiencing them being closed off. Some of the best stuff that goes on in church is in the basement during AA meetings. That is where the real stuff is being discussed, where people pour out their hearts and confess. That's what we're doing at MCS—providing a place of connection to talk about real stuff, overcoming our self-imposed and society-imposed limitations, and learning how to live in truth every day.

One of my assistants, Madison, says MCS classes are 80 percent watching and 20 percent action. The powerful change in energy and physicality of actors when they give up their old habits is so attractive.

There is always an interesting person in each of my classes: someone who has a life they were supposed to have, but then they realize they are an artist or have always wanted to try acting but never did. You may be married and become a dentist and thought that's what you wanted. Or maybe you have been acting as a lawyer or plumber, but now you want to be a stage or film actor. For those people, acting is their second career, but their first love. I want those people to express themselves without being concerned about self-development, having healthy habits, and being on a good emotional track. I go deep when it comes to unblocking people. However, you have to be open to transformation. I'm not going to promise to transform you—that is something you have control over yourself. I merely provide you the opportunity.

I have a woman in my class, Christine, who I went to SUNY New Paltz with. She has three kids and is super talented. She was always trying to be a singer and an actress and then put it all on hold. Now she is back. She has a lot of guilt about being back and about taking time off and having a family. She feels like she has to decide between one or the other. And I love that kind of person. I want that kind of person to pick up my book. Someone who used to be an actor or artist who fell out of acting when the focus of their life became about business or success. Later, they feel disappointed by this career, and now they're ready to get back to it.

In MCS, those who come to my class are usually local creatives or artists. I have had many students who wanted to use acting as a tool to help them socially and mentally. I do seminars all the time at Soho House, a membership club for creative folks working in the arts. In these seminars, I show them that my class is a way to use acting as a form of self-expression and finding your own voice. I have had so many interesting producers, non-actors, and actors who ended up registering at MCS to begin their artistic journey. I hope to one day cross paths with you as well.

Maybe you are like me and spent the first half of your life using your imagination to escape your world—let's now use your imagination to create a better one.

ABOUT THE AUTHOR

(Photo credit: Oscar Vera)

MATTHEW COROZINE, BA in theatre arts (concentration in acting and directing) SUNY New Paltz, is a multi-hyphenated creative rockstar. Not only an actor, director, producer, and teacher, Matthew is also the founding artistic director and creator of Matthew Corozine Studio (MCS), which just celebrated its 21st anniversary. Matthew has spent his years in show business unfolding his vision of a collaborative, expansive, and supportive artistic community for artists to build their craft with honor and integrity. He is one of New York City's leading Meisner-based acting coaches, teaching and creating opportunities for students to "get outta your head" in order to build a meaningful life with art. With an established student base in NYC and Washington DC (in-person) and internationally (via online coaching), MCS has expanded to Miami with in-person classes. Over the years, Matthew has coached actors and performers on Broadway, TV, film, including platinum-selling *America's Got Talent* finalist Jackie Evancho. Most recently, Matthew directed Nick Payne's play *Constellations* at MCS produced under the AEA mini contract. Matthew directed the original show *Going Through Life with No Direction* at 54 Below (NYC), produced by Alicia Keys. Matthew resides in Miami and NYC with his partner Alain and his dog Mimmo.

RUOCHEN SHEN is a storyteller and artist based in New York City. Her writings involve her observations and theories derived from acting. She creates transdisciplinary works that blur the boundary between performance and everyday life. Holding a BA in Performance Studies from NYU Tisch School of the Arts, Ruochen has a research background in experimental theatre and critical theory. Her undergraduate thesis is on the nightmarish effect of digital performances. She co-wrote and produced the original student-written play *Boba Club* in 2019 and had leading roles in several student films. Ruochen currently receives her voice and acting training in New York and has Mr. Corozine as her acting coach.

www.ingramcontent.com/pod-product-compliance
Lightning Source LLC
Chambersburg PA
CBHW020909080526
44589CB00011B/512